SURRENDER THE OUTCOME

The Path to an Impactful Life of Coaching,
Leading, and Living

BROOK CUPPS

DEDICATION

To the tough, the passionate, the unified,
and the thankful.

FOREWORD

I first met Brook Cupps a few years ago when he invited me to speak to the students of his leadership class at Centerville High School. As a proud alum, I happily said yes. On the morning of the speaking engagement, we met in person for the first time. Immediately, I was impressed by his quiet confidence, and respect shown to him by all students and faculty. Throughout the course of my day at school, I heard many "Coach Cupps" stories...All were about how he had gone out of his way to help people.

As I got to know him, I found Brook to be humble, curious, kind, thoughtful, and purposeful. Interestingly enough, he never mentioned that he was helping coach the North Coast Blue Chips AAU basketball team—the same team that LeBron James Jr. played on. He never mentioned that he sat on the bench *directly next to LeBron James* regularly. He told me he enjoyed coaching his son Gabe, was proud of his daughter Ally showing cows, and loved his wife Betsy very much, but never bragged about Gabe's status as the premier prospect in the state of Ohio. I learned all of that later, from others. For the most part, Brook lets his actions do the talking.

Brook has worked hard on this book with the intention to help you, the reader, become a more values-based leader. What you can't know, but I do, is how he embodies the values he's woven into it.

Brook is as **tough** as they come. He *always* shows up with positive body language, ready to take the fight to his opponent. He's **passionate** about what he does, always willing to do extra work—such as his "breakfast club" workouts at Centerville High School, where 20-30 students gather in the gym at 6:00 a.m., six days a week, to work on their game. He is **unified**, speaking and acting with urgency. He doesn't flinch during big moments and always has his team ready to go. Brook is constantly showing he is **thankful** for what he has, which inspires me. He relentlessly shows love to those around him, such as the personalized handshakes he creates with students or the thoughtful, handwritten thank-you notes he writes daily.

Brook has a unique goal-setting process. Rather than set outcome-related goals, he believes in *process-oriented* goals. The goal for his 2020-2021 basketball team wasn't about winning; it was, *"Attack every opportunity with purpose."* In the state championship game, his team had the ball up by one point with

15 seconds to go. They turned the ball over, giving their opponent a chance to take the lead and win the title.

In the huddle before the last possession of the game, Brook said to his team, "This is an opportunity to get it (defensive) stop. Let's attack it with purpose." They did—and Centerville High School won the first ever boys' basketball state championship. Brook and his team focused on their goal; the score took care of itself. Brook has built a culture that surrenders the outcome and is committed to the process.

BC is one of my favorite people, and he's only scratched the surface of the impact he's going to have on leaders all over the world.

Read this book and put it into action. Take notes, make an action plan, and work to live your values as well as Brook does. His message can change your life—if you're willing to do the hard work to declare what you value most and live a life where your actions prove your words.

Ryan Hawk
Author: *WELCOME TO MANAGEMENT*
Host of *The Learning Leader Show*

CONTENTS

INTRODUCTION

"The easiest person to deceive is one's own self."
–Edward George Bulwer-Lytton

People of purpose appear in all walks of life, though they are rare. It has nothing to do with money, title, or status. There are waiters and custodians who live with intentionality and purpose, just as there are presidents and CEOs that do.

For those aspiring to lead and to lead effectively, understanding one's purpose must precede any true attempt at leadership. This book lays out the framework for you to create your own intentional life of purpose in your chosen profession and in your life, starting with the story of how Mick, a basketball coach, discovered his own.

This process will be a challenge, as it should be. You are changing your life, and the life everyone you touch, from this point forward.

Hal Boyle said, "What makes a river so restful to people is that it doesn't have any doubt. It is sure to get where it is going, and it doesn't want to go anywhere else." The same can be true for you.

Trust the process. Surrender the outcome.

ChopChop!

bc

SURRENDER THE OUTCOME

THE PATH TO AN IMPACTFUL LIFE OF COACHING, LEADING, AND LIVING

"Don't ask yourself what the world needs.
Ask yourself what makes you come alive, and then go do that.
Because what the world needs are people who have come alive."
—Harold Thurman

THE STORY

CHAPTER ONE

THE POPCORN

"Man cannot remake himself without suffering,
for he is both the marble and the sculptor."
−Alexis Carrel

B abysitting: that's what I called it when Lette left me home with the kids.

Granted, they were my kids, too, but in my mind, it was still something standing in the way of me doing what I wanted, 'needed' to do. As most three- and seven-year-olds do, Dax and Rachel were constantly beckoning for my attention. "Daddy, watch this..." was easily the most common request, which usually got my attention on the third or fourth try. That is, if you would consider 'my attention' a quick glimpse up from my laptop where I was locked into the game film, the scouting report, and the next day's practice schedule. This wasn't an unusual scene at our house, but having been scouting two nights that week, this was the first night I was home before they were in bed, so their chirps for my attention were a little stronger and more frequent than normal. A little popcorn and their favorite movie, *The Friendly Dinosaur*, finally did the trick, and gave me about 15 minutes of peaceful, focused work time. But that's where it ended and my recognition for a need to change began.

The popcorn hung in the air, an attempt to make the moment linger in my mind as long as possible, I suppose. The clang of the silver metal bowl bouncing off the hardwood floor was deafening. I had no idea these sounds and smells would stay with me for ten-plus years. Dax and Rachel were both tired, and sitting down and watching a movie would usually help them fall asleep. Dax was out in the first five minutes, tipped over on the coach and dead asleep. That wasn't the case for Rachel. She had always had trouble going to sleep, and tonight was no exception. After about fifteen minutes of the movie, Rachel started to cry because she couldn't go to sleep. I didn't look up from my computer—hoping it would take care of itself, I guess. She finally got up off the couch and just stood in the middle of the living room, crying and holding her popcorn.

Rage flooded over me. I jumped out of my chair, knocking everything on my lap—papers, notebook, computer—to the floor. In one swoop, I swatted the popcorn bowl out of Rachel's hands and into the air. It crashed to the ground, scattering popcorn all over the living room floor. I snagged the bowl on its first bounce off the ground and slammed it back against the hardwood floor. "Stop crying!" served as my only condolence for her. I turned and walked out of the living room and into the kitchen, leaving Rachel to calm herself, so I could continue serving my needs. At this point, she had melted to the floor, sobbing.

In the kitchen, I paced with the angst of a criminal at large. I sat the dented popcorn bowl on the counter and headed back into the living room. As I turned the corner, Rachel sat up and began drying her own tears from her face. The rage that had flooded me before immediately turned to shame. My heart melted.

Questions zipped through my head: *What was I thinking? How could I blow up over something so trivial? What is wrong with me?* I was at a loss for words. All I could say was "I'm sorry." I hurried over to pick her up, praying I hadn't been so stupid that she would never forget this experience. I whispered "Sorry" another 10 times as I held her and kissed her head.

Rachel didn't deserve that. She hadn't done anything a normal seven-year-old doesn't do from time to time. That moment, standing in my living room holding Rachel in my arms, I found a clarity of awareness in myself I had never experienced. The man I was became crystal clear. I was lost. And the man I wanted to be began to come to light. Although this was the bottom for me, it would be another five years before I had the courage to become the person and coach I wanted to be.

CHAPTER TWO

LETTE LOWERS THE BOOM

*"The spirit is larger than the body. The body is pathetic
compared to what we have inside us."*
–Diana Nyad

I'd had all I could take. Head down, fuming, I stormed off the court, clearly frustrated. I usually meet with my assistants before talking to my team, but not today. I headed straight for the locker room and began ripping into our guys before most of them could even find their seats.

"I've been a head high school basketball coach for 10 years and I've never seen anything close to as pathetic as that effort was tonight! What a joke. We practice all year to come out here and go through the motions? On senior night, of all times?! We have guys in this locker room that think they should be starting, just hoping for the guy in front of them to screw up so they get a chance to play. Think about that. How bad of a teammate are you if you are rooting against one of your own teammates? Unbelievable!"

I took a breath and glared around the room, attempting to make eye contact with every player. Most had their heads down and were desperately avoiding my death stare.

"Pick your heads up. We're not going to come in here and talk about not playing hard, not caring about each other. You had a choice tonight. You chose to not rebound, to not get in a defensive stance, to not execute our offense, and to not share the ball. That was your choice, not mine, nor any of your other coaches. Yours!"

Now I was on a roll.

"This group is full of two things. The first is potential; we have one senior and several talented underclassmen who've won championship after championship in youth and middle school. Apparently, you haven't figured out that varsity teams don't have your middle school highlights saved on their phones!"

The lone senior on our West Lake team was a scrawny little 5'8" guard who never played unless the game was well out of reach. He was a good kid, but he fell into the same category as everyone else regarding his role on the team: he cared more about his playing time than anything going on with the team. Senior leadership is precious to a coach, because a lack of it is destructive to a team.

"The second thing this team has plenty of is entitlement. You and your parents are never happy with your position or role on the team. If you start on the JV team, you should be playing varsity. If you are on the varsity team, you should be starting. If you are starting, you should be getting more shots. The only reason I don't have a meeting after practice every day is because I won't talk to parents about playing time. If I did, I would have a line waiting outside my door every night! The record of the team doesn't even matter. It's all about you. This is what you get when everything is about you. Practice is Monday after school. See you then."

I stormed out of the locker room. I was headed to the coaches' office, a short walk down the hallway. Head down, I hadn't taken more than three steps towards the office before things went sideways.

"Coach Mick, you got a minute?"

I looked up. It was the dad of our starting forward. This guy was the perfect example of what I had just said in the locker room. He was only happy if his son had scored 20 points, never mind whether the team had just won or lost. It was all about his son.

"Nah, we're not talking right now, man," I replied.

I was already frustrated, but instead of keeping my head down and avoiding any further confrontation, I decided to take the tough guy route, and lock eyes with him as we passed. He stopped just as I walked past him.

"Yeah, that's convenient, isn't it. You're a clown. Nice job tonight, Coach," he retorted.

My emotions were under control until his sarcastic comment hit, and when it did, I started to turn around to go back towards him. Fortunately, my two assistant coaches were close enough to stop me from doing something stupid that I would regret.

In the office, the meeting with the coaches was pretty much as it had been all season. We talked about how bad the team was defensively and how poorly we executed offensively. We talked about which players performed well and which players had not; obviously, the latter list was much longer on that night. A few of the assistant coaches offered basketball suggestions and adjustments we could have made, such as going to a zone because we got beat off the dribble so much, or going to our sets offensively more to try and create some consistent offense. None of those really seemed like the answer. Finally, one assistant offered a thought that appealed and made sense.

"I just don't think it matters what we say or do until our guys care. Right now, they don't care about anything but themselves.

Until that changes, the results aren't changing. You say all the time that this is their team. Well, it's their team and it's their choice. Until they choose the team over themselves, nothing else matters," he said.

Lette, my wife, stuck her head into the coaches' office to let me know that she was heading home with Chubs, our four-year-old son. His real name was Dax, but his fat, chubby cheeks led to our guys calling him Chubs most of the time. Our daughter, however, wanted to ride home with me from the game. Rachel—I called her Dink—loved being with me. She drew plays, kept shot charts on scouting trips, and even watched films of games and practice sessions with me. Picture little Sheryl Yoast, daughter of Coach Yoast in *Remember the Titans*. That was Dink to a T. If you have ever seen the movie, she was a clone of Coach Yoast's daughter.

From what I noticed when I was around the house, Chubs was a pretty good little kid. He didn't cry much, and was always entertaining himself. We would spend a little time in the basement some weekends as he learned how to dribble and shoot using his mini-hoop. I thought he liked basketball at the time, but I realize now it was likely that he was just enjoying time with his dad.

At this time in her life, Dink loved two things: cows and the West Lake basketball team. She never had any desire to play basketball, but she never missed a game. Her passion for cows came from her mother. Lette grew up on a big dairy farm, and introduced Dink to the cows when she was little. It was pretty much over from there. She thought of cows like the average person thinks of a dog, and she treated them that way. If Dink wasn't in the house, there was a 100% chance she was sitting in a stall talking to one of her cows. Her love for animals certainly carried over to people. Dink always looked for the best in people, and she expected the same back in return. She expected the best from my players, too. After games, she had lots of questions, and this car ride home was no different.

"Why didn't you play Alex more? I think he's a good shooter."

"Your guys should've rebounded better. Don't you think that would've helped, Dad?"

"How come Mark turned the ball over so much?"

"Why did you guys look so tired?"

Her questions gradually faded with each of my weak, short, haphazard answers. My goal was to get her to stop asking me questions after games. On that particular night, I was successful more quickly than usual. She stopped asking questions, turning her eyes sadly towards the car window and watching the fields pass by.

I have a lot of regrets from my early coaching days, and being short with my loved ones during stressful occasions stings the most. I'm embarrassed and disappointed when I think of all the opportunities I missed with my family. I became caught up in winning games, because winning games meant we were better than our opponents—I was better—and losing was just unacceptable.

When we finally got home, Dink and I walked in the front door to find the living room completely destroyed. Chubs' toys were all over the place. There were plates and cups from lunch on the end table by the couch and dirty clothes left lying on the floor by the recliner, and I snapped.

"What the hell happened here? Why is this place such a disaster? Dax, clean up your toys. Rachel, your clothes to the laundry room, *now*."

I started grabbing dirty dishes and made a show of slamming them into the kitchen sink. My wife was not amused.

"Rachel, Dax, put that stuff down. Come on, it's been a long day. Off to bed. We'll spend time with Daddy tomorrow when he's calmed down," Lette said.

Lette knew the drill. She had seen it all before. We started dating in high school, and have been together ever since. So, that's 16 years of experience around me and my coaching to draw from. She's a veteran. After a loss, stay the hell away from me, no matter the opponent or how well we might have played. After a win, celebrate, no matter the opponent or how poorly we might have played. It was a rollercoaster ride, but she was an expert in managing it.

Lette is as tough as they come. She's not scared of work and she's not afraid to tell you what she thinks. She grew up the oldest of three, the only girl in her family. She spent her time as a kid outside helping out on the family farm—milking cows, usually. A dairy farmer at heart, married to a basketball coach, she is a saint. Lette is easygoing most of the time, often choosing to sit back and observe—that is, until her kids are involved. If Dink or Chubs is in the mix, Lette is going to tell you what she thinks, and when she's finished, you will know with crystal clear clarity where she stands on the matter.

Rachel and Dax came over to give me a hug. I gave each a half-hearted squeeze in return, and off to bed they went. I immediately pulled out my laptop and started watching that night's game. The film—which was awful, by the way—wasn't what made this night stand out, though. After I had watched about 20 minutes of game film, Lette came back downstairs. This in itself wasn't unusual. There were a lot of nights she would come back downstairs to watch a movie or sit and talk with me. This trip downstairs didn't feel as casual.

"Mick, we need to talk." There was a preciseness to her voice that got my attention. "Something has to change."

"What do you mean?" I thought I knew where she was going, but was oblivious to how deep she would go.

"You have to change. I'm not doing this anymore. *We* are not doing this anymore," she said, pointing upstairs to the kids' rooms. "You lose a basketball game and then won't talk to your daughter, won't come home and play with your son? They just want to spend time with their dad. They don't care if you win or lose. They don't care if you're the best coach in the world or the dumbest to ever sit on the sideline. They care that you're their dad, and they just want to spend time with you. You leave the house at 5:00 am and get back at 7:00 pm every day from November through March. Then, the little time you have with them, you waste by being mad about something that happened at practice or in the game. That's not their fault and it's not my fault. More importantly, we don't care, because that has absolutely nothing to do with why we love you."

Now she was on a roll.

"And while we're at it, Mick, stop feeling sorry for yourself, like you're this helpless victim. You act like everything that happens with the team is the players' fault. 'They don't want it, they aren't bought in, they don't care.' Aren't you the coach? Isn't that your job? I've heard you quote Jocko Willink a thousand times— 'There's no such thing as a bad team, only bad leaders.' Guess who the leader of your program is? Not the captain of your teams. It's you. Or how about, 'What you see is what you coached' or 'You get what you allow'? You can't say that stuff to your players and then not own it yourself. I don't need to know that much about basketball to tell you your problem isn't basketball. See you in the morning."

She couldn't help but throw one more jab in on her way back upstairs.

"Oh, and feel free to pick up the toys and start the laundry before you come to bed," she quipped.

CHAPTER THREE

THE FLAT TASTE OF A SEASON'S END

"It's not what you look at that matters; it's what you see."
–Henry David Thoreau

P rior to this season, this team had set goals: sweep our rivals, Bentonville; win the conference; and make it to the District Finals. Dreams of the first goal were destroyed in the second week of the season, when Bentonville blew us out by 25 points on their home floor. We really struggled on the road, but not nearly as much as we struggled on Tuesday nights. We managed to win only one Tuesday night game all season, going a pitiful 1-6 on that particular day of the week. Smaller crowds, and not as much hype as a Friday night game, was a bad combination for a team that struggled to compete consistently. That being said, we were never in the league race, so we never even sniffed making it to conference. That left the final goal—West Lake making it to the District Finals—the only one left we could achieve.

We finished the regular season an unimpressive 8-12, and we didn't even play that well. On paper, this team could have won 15 games. We were lucky to win the eight that we did, and pulled two of those out in the final seconds.

Prior to the high school tournament, all the area coaches meet to vote for tournament seeds. We vote on every team in our sectional (or local area) that is in the tournament. Fortunately, every team gets into the tournament in our state. Our area coaches recognized our mediocrity, voting West Lake the 10th seed out of 18 teams.

After a subpar season, the guys did pull it together for the tournament. In our first game, we played our best basketball of the season. We were unselfish and moved the ball on offense, contested shots, and rebounded on defense. We cruised to a 10-point win over the sixth-seeded team. It was an upset based on seeding, but a team we should have beaten based on pure talent.

The second game was a completely different story. It was a grind. Both teams had trouble scoring and the game felt like it took four hours to play. Based on the score, I wish I could tell you that one of the teams held the ball, but that wasn't the case. It was just two bad teams being bad. We squeaked out a 30-28 win over the 12th seed.

In our third game, the sectional final, we expected to be playing the best team and first seed, Clarksville. But they suffered an upset in the second round, making our path to the Districts easier—or so we thought. We were matched up with Scranton, a team we had beaten by 12 points just two weeks earlier.

Honestly, I don't remember too much about the Sectional Final. In terms of performance, we played somewhere between the quality shown during our first and second game: not great, but not awful. Fortunately, their best player had rolled his ankle in their previous game, and saw limited minutes against us. We ended up pulling the game out in the fourth quarter for a 52-45 win.

The game that still sits clearly in my mind is the District game. Having achieved our goal by reaching that milestone, we had all but mailed in the rest of the season.

During that week of practice, three of the guys turned up late to practice and one player was supposedly sick and unable to train. I say supposedly because although he said he was sick, I didn't believe him. Two students I had in class told me they had seen this same player at the shopping mall the night he couldn't practice. On top of that, one of our starters had been diagnosed—by his dad—with an ankle sprain, so he missed a day of practice.

The practice sessions themselves were lackluster at best. The energy was low and our coaches spent all of their time yelling at guys to talk to each other and play harder. Passing was sloppy and execution on offense was non-existent. On defense, we had no attention to boxing out and rebounding. It was as if we hadn't been practicing for four months. To say they were uninspired would be a drastic understatement.

On paper, we should have expected to win the game. Our players were just as good as theirs. We had more size and athleticism for sure, but everyone knows that doesn't always equate to winning. On the floor, it wasn't even close. They jumped on us from the opening tip and never looked back. We were down 15-3 at the end of the first quarter, and it never got better. We looked exactly like the team from practice all week. I called two timeouts in the first quarter, but it didn't matter. Our opponents were playing their best basketball of the season, and we were not. They took the ball from us on defense and scored at will on offense. By half-time, it was a 20 point game, 34-14. There was really no point in yelling. Deep down, I think I was about as glad to see the season ending as they looked like they were. The second half was more of the same; we never made it a game. The final score ended up being 67-37, but it wasn't that close.

After the game, the locker room felt different. Guys were crying, like they always do when the season ends, but several guys just changed their clothes and walked out as soon as I had finished talking. No "thank you" hugs for the seniors, no consoling teammates. Players just changed clothes and walked out. I remember playing on teams that gave everything they had to their teammates—no jealousy, no backstabbing, no hate—just love and support. I wasn't sure how that felt as a coach; I had never truly experienced it. But one thing I knew for sure: it didn't feel like this.

CHAPTER FOUR

DAD TALKS TURKEY

"What good are wings without the courage to fly?"
–Atticus Finch in To Kill A Mockingbird, *by Harper Lee*

I usually have no trouble sleeping at night, but following a loss like we'd just experienced and the season I had just survived, it wasn't too surprising that my eyes popped open at 3:30 am and refused to close. I stayed in bed for a few minutes before getting up and going out to the kitchen. I had been struggling for most of the season to understand why I committed so much time to being frustrated and angry. Since the talk with Lette, that question was even stronger and louder in my head. Now that the season was finally over, it was time to find an answer.

A phone call at 3:45 am would seem weird to 99% of the people in the world, but a call to my dad at that time of the morning was equivalent to a lunch-time check-in. He would answer, and sound like he was halfway through his day. I suspect there were plenty of times he was actually asleep, but you would never know it from his upbeat tone.

Dad—the Silver Fox as he was known to his former students, because of his full white head of hair—was a retired high school physics teacher and baseball coach. That doesn't come close to giving you a full understanding of who he is, though, so let me provide more perspective.

Dad grew up as the oldest of three boys. His dad was an abusive alcoholic and often beat my Grandma. That alcoholism led to Grandpa not being able to keep a job, so the family was very poor. They constantly had to move because they could never pay their rent. Dad attended 24 different high schools, and when he finally graduated, he decided to enlist in the Air Force. Dad knew that was the only way he would ever be able to go to college. He served four years in the Air Force and earned a teaching degree before he married my Mom. There is much more to tell about my dad, but suffice it to say that he epitomizes humility, hard work, and sacrifice.

The early morning call became a 15-minute drive over to dad's house to talk about my job, my family, and my life. I started the conversation off with the questions that had been burning inside of me for several weeks.

"I just don't know if I can coach these kids. They're different now—so much entitlement—and so lazy. They won't put their phones down long enough to even let you coach them. They don't listen and they don't even understand what playing hard looks like. They're clueless," I ranted.

Dad just sat and listened as I continued to unload.

"And don't get me started on their parents. Holy crap, Dad, they're unbelievable. Nothing ever satisfies them. They're never happy. Nothing I do as a coach pleases them. There is no concept of the team. It's all about their son, and they refuse to let their child struggle and figure something out on his own. They are always trying to swoop in and save them from anything that might hurt their feelings, or, God forbid, make them better. I just don't know if this is all worth it. I mean, why do it? Why put myself through this? For what? What's the pay off?" I continued.

By this time, Dad was leaning back in his recliner, staring out the window, petting his dog on his lap. He let some time pass and began to speak while continuing to gaze outside.

"Why *do* you coach, Mick?" he asked calmly.

The question caught me off guard, and the simplicity of it stumped me. I tried responding quickly, though I would later realize just how deep this question was.

"I don't know... because I love basketball. The game was great to me, so I want to give back to the game," I replied.

Dad turned to look at me, making eye contact.

"That sounds like a great answer, but it doesn't say anything. What's that mean, you love the game? Growing up, you loved Connect 4, but you're not coaching that. You loved riding your bike and jumping over mulch piles when you were in middle school, but you're not coaching that. There's a lot of things to love in this world. You're making the decision to use the single life you've been given to do one thing. You better make sure that one thing you choose is worthy of that one life. Now, why do you coach?"

He had me rattled now. I had no idea where to go from here. I pressed my thumbs into my temples, dropped my head, and gave the best answer I could think of.

"I have no idea," I responded. At that moment, reality smacked me in the face like a frying pan. I had come to talk to Dad for him to help me figure out who to blame for my team's lack of performance, and the answer was becoming painstakingly clear. It was me.

Dad came back at me. "Come on. Think. Why do you coach? What are you talking about with giving back to the game?

What's basketball given you? It's given you some great memories you never want to forget, and it's given you some feelings you never want to remember. Has the game really been that great to you? I mean, it's a game—it's not inherently positive or negative any more than ping-pong, going on a walk, or spending time with friends would be. The greatness from each of those comes from you—how you view the experience, how you embrace the opportunity. Too many people get caught up thinking like everyone else—the glass is either half full or half empty. That doesn't matter. The glass just is what it is. The only thing that matters is that you realize you're the one holding the pitcher. When you realize that, you can pour as much water as you want into any glass you want."

Ideas were starting to come to me now. I began to reflect on the relationships I had had with teammates and coaches growing up, and the bonds I had formed with the players on the first few teams I had coached. The coaches in my life were the most influential people to me, outside of my parents. I wanted to have the same impact on other kids that my coaches had on me. I coached to help kids realize their potential.

I believe that sports are a microcosm of the world. The same could be said about music, art, and academia, but it was sports for me. Nothing was a better instigator of growth. I know basketball, so that's my choice, but I was realizing the game is just the platform I was using. It alone was not my purpose.

"I want to help kids grow, I want to challenge them, I want to help them be better than they think they can be. It doesn't even have to be basketball. I coach the game because I know it and enjoy it, but that's not why I coach. I coach to make a difference in the life of kids," I said.

Dad was smiling now. "Yes, now we're making progress. That's good. You could do that as a teacher, as a parent, as a doctor, as a babysitter, as a football coach, baseball coach, or basketball coach. What you do isn't nearly as important as why you do it. We're getting closer to your purpose."

He could see the answer clearly before I even knew what I was looking for, but his questions led me right to it. "What did you like so much about playing backyard football with your brother when you were growing up?" he asked.

Now he was tapping into some of my favorite memories. Every Sunday, my brother and his friends would play football in a neighbor's yard. I must have begged for a year before my brother would let me go with him. Jimmy is seven years older than me, so his friends were much bigger than me, too, and there was no flag or two-hand touch in those days. It was full-blown tackle football, and I absolutely loved it. I made sure nothing ever interfered with Sunday afternoon football. I chuckled as I started to respond to Dad's question.

"Ha! I did love that. I know one of the things I loved, which I know I've never told Jimmy, was the car ride with just the two of us. On the way back, we would talk about the best plays from the game we had just played. I remember my confidence surging when he brought up how great one of my catches was. I took a lot of pride in being the youngest and smallest, but never backing down from trying to tackle guys six, seven, eight years older than me. That was fun to me. I was always fighting to prove myself. I might not have always been successful by the outcome or score, but I knew if I had done my best. I liked that feeling."

Dad nodded. "I guess I never even thought about the time you guys got to spend together. Of course that's a great memory. Jimmy was always really good to you when you were little. He put up with a lot of crap from you and never complained about dragging his little brother along with him."

"I think the second part of that is important to your purpose," Dad continued. "Your *why* is the thing that gets your blood going, what gets you excited. It's the thing that makes you want to get up in the morning. It's sad to see how many people live such unintentional, uninspired lives. They spend all their time focused on what they want to do, and very little on why they are doing it. If they only knew that once they discover their *why*, they can apply that to any profession or aspect of life. Knowing your *why* makes you a better doctor, bus driver, salesman, teacher, anything you want. For you, Mick, that underdog mentality is at the heart of who you are. It showed up over and over when you were a kid, going to park after park to find the best pick-up games that made you a better player. Your early-morning shooting workouts were really just your way of saying, 'I may not be as big or as athletic, but I'm going to be as good as I possibly can be by being super skilled and in the best shape possible.'"

He paused and smiled. "What were your favorite movies growing up? Right, all the Rocky movies. You loved the underdog. Heck, you always picked the scrawniest Christmas trees as your favorite. You've always worked really hard to be the best version of yourself that you could be. And that's always been enough for you. I admire your ability to dismiss other people's verdict on determining your success or failure."

Pssshhh. Geez. Dad was giving me insight into who I was that would've taken me weeks to discover on my own. I think I would've gotten there, but it would've taken some time. I could see the pattern he was pointing out, and it resonated with me. I felt butterflies in my stomach. That was it. What he was saying was my *why*, my purpose.

Now he was coming in for the kill. "You need to figure out exactly how you want to articulate your *why*. It has to come from you, in your words. Just remember, basketball is your *what*—it's actually just one of your *whats*. Your *why*, now, that's the important one. Your *why* should resonate so deeply with you that it leaves a mark on every part of your life. It should impact how you teach, how you coach, how you parent, how you act as a brother or son, how you are as a friend. Your *why* is the sole driving force for how you do everything. These people that go around acting one way at work, another way at home, another way with their friends... they're not bad people, they just don't have that North Star. Your *why* is your North Star—so find it and allow everything else to flow from there."

Questions were ricocheting through my mind. What is my North Star, my purpose? What do I want out of life? How do I want my life to impact the people around me? I didn't know the answers, but I knew I was far closer than I had been a few hours earlier. That self-awareness alone was inspiring.

I stood up to say goodbye and give Dad a hug. Before I could get to the door, I heard Mom hollering from her bedroom. I didn't realize she was even awake, but she made sure to let me know.

"Don't you leave this house without talking to me first," she shouted.

I smiled at Dad as I headed towards her. Dad raised his eyebrows as if to say, "What'd you expect?"

CHAPTER FIVE

MOM WEIGHS IN

*"Every man and woman must form their own ethos on what
they stand for in their life. You have to stand for something,
or you stand for nothing."*
–David Goggins

Mom, never in search of words, started right in.
"Mick, you don't look good. How are ya? How are my babies?"

I hadn't even finished hugging her before she let me have it.

"Now you listen. I don't care about your ball team or school or whatever else you have going on, but I do care about those two you have at home. You lose a ball game and then act like they don't exist, or that they're this burden you have to deal with. They ain't a burden. They're your greatest gift to the world, so you better wake up and start treating them like that," she said.

"I've already heard this from Lette, Mom. I know. I need to do better at home. That would be a lot easier to do if we won a few basketball games. But I know, either way, I need to do better," I replied.

She wasn't done.

"You're wasting time, son. Stop wasting time with them. I watch you when you're with them. Sometimes you're smiling and enjoying it, then other times you're calculating how much longer you have to play tractors or dolls before you can go do something you want to do."

That comment probably stung more than anything else she could say. Talk about self-awareness. This was medicine I was not mentally prepared for. That definitely wasn't who I wanted to be, but clearly, it's who I was. She had more after that.

"This ain't about you, Mick. All that moping and pouting after you lose, that's you trying to make it about you. Not talking to anyone after you lose a little old basketball game, that's making it about you. Treating your time with your family as less important than your time watching film or at practice, that's making it about you. You can act like you're putting in all this time for your kids—and I know some of that is true for you, you do care about them—but be honest with yourself. Most of the time you put in is for you, to help you elevate your status, where you rank as a coach, to improve what other people think about you."

"Why do you think you're so upset when you lose?" She went on mercilessly. "It's not because you're hurting for your team. It's because you're *embarrassed*. In your mind it means that the other team is better than you. Their players are better, their coach is better, their practices are better. It's all just nonsense. Those ball games don't mean anything."

"You've lost focus on what's important, and it's not good for anyone—not for you, your players, and especially not for your family. Now either knock it off or go do something else."

I had gotten plenty of 'straighten-up' talks from Mom over the years, but none quite like this one. I had a million things running through my head. I went straight to the big three victim defenses.

- Blaming: This isn't my fault!
- Complaining: You'd think you could at least get a little support from your own mom.
- Defending: I work my butt off and this is the thanks I get?

Wisely, instead of trying to defend myself, I decided to keep it short.

"Ok, Mom. Ok. I don't think I've been *that* bad. Sure, I need to fix some stuff like everyone else, but I don't think I'm much different than every other coach out there."

With that, she glared through my soul with a look only your mom can give you to let you know she's disappointed in you. Then she hit me with the knock-out punch.

"Exactly," she said, as she kissed me on the forehead and walked towards the kitchen.

That tongue-lashing hurt, but it did bring some urgency to what Dad had shared with me. Mom was one of the most positive, caring, loving people in the world. She would literally do anything for anyone. She was a servant in every sense of the word. Dad and Jimmy had told me about her mean streak, though. I don't remember seeing it growing up, but clearly anything impacting her grandkids was a major trigger, and she had definitely gotten my attention.

I made another round of goodbyes, telling Mom and Dad thanks for taking the time to talk to me, and gave them both another hug. Before I could get to the door, Mom stopped me again.

"I have one more thing I just thought of."

"You weren't fast enough," Dad said with a chuckle and a grin.

"Papaw Reggie was just a farmhand his whole life, you know that, right?" Mom said.

I didn't know a lot about my Papaw's life, but I did know he worked for a farmer and he would always ask me if I wanted to go hunting with him. That was about it.

"Yeah," I replied, not sure where this one was going.

"Well, here's a little story he told me when I was probably 12 years old," Mom said.

One sunny morning, a little girl with ratty shorts and a long, baggy shirt was marching down the beach. Starfish had washed up on the beach the night before, and she was flinging them back into the ocean. This morning, there were far more than normal, but the little girl was unwavering in her mission. One after the other, she picked up her five- legged friends, muttered something under her breath, and sent it flying back into the ocean, back to life.

A businessman happened to be walking down the beach at the same time, in search of a little fresh air and a break from the hustle and bustle of his job. The girl's actions caught the man's eye far before he reached her. As they got closer, the man realized what the young girl was doing. He looked down and scoffed under his breath, as if to say, "What a waste of time. She can never get all those starfish back out into the ocean." The man continued on, careful to avoid the stranded starfish. As the man approached, the little girl noticed him. She saw his fancy outfit and the cut-throat look in his eyes, neither of which mattered to her. She continued on her mission, and neither made eye contact as their paths crossed. The man, now in starfish-free sand thanks to the little girl, stopped, turned back, and shouted at her.

"You're wasting your time, you know. No matter how long you stay out here, there will always be more starfish stranded. Even if you throw all the ones on this beach back in, they'll just be more tomorrow. You're really not making a difference at all." The girl, now irritated with being interrupted, stared the man down as she took a few steps towards him, starfish in hand. "Really?" she shouted back. Never breaking eye contact, she flung another back into the ocean, back to life. "I made a difference for that one."

The story brought a grin to my face. It gave me clarity.

Mom continued, "Son, you've always been about saving whatever starfish you can save. Don't let the world change that. Don't give in to what everyone else does. Be different. It's easy in this life to spend so much time thinking about what you don't have, what we can't do, that we forget about all of our blessings and the things we can do, the people we can help. The little girl decides that she is not going to allow what she can't do keep her from doing what she can do. She can save the starfish on her beach that morning, so that's what she does. The fact that she can't save all the starfish on the whole beach, or that they could end up right back there in the morning, doesn't matter. She's focused on doing what she can, not what she can't.

"What you do matters, Mick, as a father, a husband, and coach. It may not matter to everyone, but to the kids in your house and on your team, you are as important as anyone else in their lives. Don't walk by any more starfish."

"I got it, Mom. Thank you," I replied.

She kissed me again on the top of the cheek and I walked out of the door. Thanks to Mom and Dad, I was definitely in a better place and more aware of myself. I still had questions to answer, but I could feel energy and possibility. I could feel hope in the difference I might be able to make. I was as excited as I had been in a long time. I wasn't exactly sure where I was going, but I was ready for wherever this awakening was going to lead.

As I drove away, I beat myself up a little. My parents had had this wisdom to offer me all my life, and I just hadn't heard it before. Thinking back, I could see times when they had tried to teach me all of this. I just hadn't been ready. Maybe it's true what they say: "When the student is ready, the teacher will appear."

CHAPTER SIX

FINDING MY PURPOSE

"It's your road, and yours alone.
Others may walk it with you, but no one can walk it for you."
–Rumi

I've always enjoyed the off-season. The feeling of starting new with a clean slate was refreshing. I liked the opportunity to make changes based on the mental notes I had made the year before. Change never really scared me; it just seemed like a necessary part of life. Is there anything more fundamental to life than change?

But this off-season was different. I had experienced these small come-to-Jesus talks before, but I had always just fallen back to the way I'd done things in the past. I would start off with these grand illusions of how I was going to change everything about how I coached and how our team played, but by December, we were right back to being just like everyone else. This year, I was determined to make the change and coach my team the way I thought coaching should be handled. If being confronted by three of the most important people in my life couldn't get me going in the right direction, what could?

I spent the next several weeks thinking, writing down ideas, and reading about outstanding leaders in all areas of life. All of them had such clarity. They knew exactly who they were and what they stood for. They had a system that they not only believed, but that they lived by. They didn't waiver from that value system, because it was at the core of who they were. They lived their *why*.

I had pages and pages of notes on everything that mattered to me: values I believed in, values I thought I actually lived by, and values I wanted to live by. I had a ton of values on those lists that I thought were important, like hard work, integrity, humility, passion, sacrifice, family, balance, toughness, courage, grit, faith, growth, gratitude, kindness, respect, and unity, to name a few. But what now? The self-reflection had been powerful, but where could I go with it? How would I find my purpose, my *why*, from all these thoughts and ideas? I was at a standstill.

When I'm stuck, one of my calls is to my old high school basketball coach, Coach Z. He was basically a basketball savant and an incredible player. An All-American in college, he played several years in the NBA with Oscar Robertson and the Cincinnati Royals. His ability to anticipate what would happen in a game always amazed me. Coach Z was a true steward of the game. I had never talked to him about this kind of stuff before; it had always been basketball stuff, like what should we do against this match-up zone or how to guard a big guy. But I had a hunch he would be able to provide some direction on this, too.

The answer was always *yes* when you called Z to ask for help. I wished I had called more often just to check in and see how he was doing.

"Coach, it's Mick. It's been awhile. How are you?" I said to him.

"Mick! Great to hear from you. How are you? How's your family?" he replied in his typically positive manner.

"I'm good, Coach. Family is doing well. How are you?" I responded.

"Oh, I'm fine. I had surgery on my knee a few weeks back, so I'm not moving around real well right now, but I'm good. You talk to any of the guys from the team anymore? Do you guys stay in touch?" he asked.

It had been over 20 years since I played high school ball under his leadership. It always warmed me that he would ask that. He still cares. Despite it being 20 years later, we were still his guys, and how we continued to view ourselves as a team still mattered to him.

"Ah, yeah, a few of them I talk to pretty regularly. I keep up with all of them, though. Most of the guys are doing well,"I said.

"Yeah, that's good. I knew they would. Great group of kids. You guys were fun to coach," he replied.

Coach paused for a moment. I pictured him flashing back and smiling about some of the characters we had on our team. He had coached for almost 40 years, but could remember every one of his guys' names and which team they played on. An incredible feat.

Coach got straight to it. "So, what can I do for ya? I know you don't call just to shoot the bull, so how can I help?"

I tried to share what was in my head as clearly as I could, which wasn't easy, because my head was still a mess!

"Well, I think I need to change. I love coaching, but I can't keep doing it the way I'm doing it. All I'm doing right now is trying to win the next game. Whatever that takes, that's what I try to do. We talk about respect, responsibility, and teamwork, but I don't know that we follow through on any of them. We're so up and down as a team, too. Our locker room has that feeling of getting along because they have to, but our guys don't really support each other. And I'm miserable. It's not fun. I'm mad all the time. Why would I want to spend the next 20 years of my life dealing with players and parents complaining about playing time and how I screw up?" I told him.

I felt like I had just backed up a giant dump truck and unloaded on him. All the progress I thought I had made over the last few weeks since my talk with Mom and Dad had been put on the shelf. I presented Coach with the raw account of my situation.

"You mentioned respect, responsibility, and teamwork. Why did you pick those three values to talk about?" he said. He always knew the answer before he asked the question.

"Because that's what we used for *our* team," he replied, answering his own question.

"You're right about one thing," he continued. It sounds like you need to change something. It's supposed to be fun. You're in the greatest profession on earth. No one else gets to shape the world the way a coach does. It's an honor, a privilege. If you're not enjoying coaching, there's very little chance your players are enjoying playing. That's a bigger problem than *you* not enjoying it. The number one thing you need to decide is, what do you want the kids on your team to get from playing for you? Whether the team wins one game or 20, whether they're the leading scorer or the last man on the bench, what do you want them to take with them? It's a pretty big question, and most coaches never take the time to answer it. For me, it was respect, responsibility, and teamwork, because those are the three most important things in my life. Those are the things I value the most. Yours will, and should, be different. You're a different person than me, with different experiences than me. Does that make sense?" he asked.

Sarcasm was one of Coach's best tools, but this was genuine.

"Yes, it does, but I don't know how I'm supposed to pick values that matter the most to me. I mean, after playing for you, I think respect, responsibility, and teamwork are pretty important. They seem as good as any other ones," I replied.

Coach replied. "That's partially true. They are as good as any other ones, but they aren't *your* answer to the question I asked: what do you want your players to learn? It has to be your answer, not mine. If it's not your answer, you will never weave those values into every part of your team and program like you need to. You will never turn to those values when things aren't going well. You will never measure your success or failure by how well your players understand and embrace those values. When they come from you—when you own them—then your accountability to those values goes through the roof. They become your filter for all decisions. It's a unique way to coach, but it's the best way—for you and for your players."

That got me thinking. This is where all that reflection and self-awareness leads: to core values that represent me and what I stand for and believe in. *I needed to find my core values.*

"I've thought about it, but I can't get it narrowed down, Coach. They all seem important. How many should I have?" I asked him.

"That's a good question. I don't think there is a right number, but there is a wrong number. Simplicity is king. Anything less than five is probably ok. Two or three would be perfect. Most coaches just let this be a luck-of-the-draw type thing that might or might not touch on the surface of a bunch of different values. But this approach lets the players and their parents know exactly what they are going to get out of being on your team, and it's not going to be some surface-level understanding of the values you pick. It's going to be a deep understanding and appreciation for them, " Coach said.

Ok. Ok. So I needed to do some soul searching and think about what was really important to me. I could do that. What did I want my players to gain from being a part of our team? Got it.

"One more thing before we get off here, Mick," Coach said. On his team, we had learned to listen up when he said "One more thing."

"When you first started, you talked about a lot of frustrations and challenges you've been facing. I just want to make sure you know that this doesn't make all of those go away. I mean, I think this is how you should approach coaching, teaching, parenting, your job... pretty much life; but those challenges are still going to be there. You're still going to get frustrated. You're still going to fail."

I was hoping he would at least finish with "...but not as much," but that never came.

"The good news is, this will help your perspective change. Right now, you think you control way more things than you can control. When you let that need for control go and realize you're way more of an observer than a controller in this world, much of that frustration will fade away. All those challenges become opportunities for your core values to shine. You'll stop dreading them and start embracing them. Without those times of adversity, when would we ever grow?"

By this time, I was taking notes. "Coach, I don't know how I can thank you enough. This has helped so much. I've got a lot of work to do, but I'm going to get it figured out. Thank you!" I said to him.

"No problem, Mick. It was great talking to you. I have no doubt you'll get it figured out. Let me know when you settle on those core values. I'll let you know if they're right!" he laughed.

I hung up thinking I wasn't sure what I did to deserve so many people in my life willing to help and patient with me until I was ready to receive it. But between my wife, my Mom, my Dad, and my coach, I was now headed in the right direction.

CHAPTER SEVEN

FINDING MY CORE VALUES: TOUGH, PASSIONATE, UNIFIED, AND THANKFUL

"Who looks outside, dreams; who looks inside, awakes."
–Carl Jung

I spent the next week or so trying to figure out exactly what I thought was important—what I wanted our players to take away from my program. After talking to Coach Z, I knew this had to come from me. If I was the leader of the program, then the values of the program needed to be central to me. Then I would stand up for them, I would fight for them, and I would turn to them when things weren't going well. But I had to do some soul-searching to know what really mattered to me.

Honestly, this was a little embarrassing. I had been coaching for 10 years, living for almost 30 years, and here I was just now trying to find out what was important to me. I'm not sure why I felt embarrassed when only Lette, Mom, Dad, and Coach Z knew about this search for myself. Nonetheless, I felt it.

Narrowing down my values was difficult. Thanks to Dad, I realized that the underdog mentality was important to me. That's how I always viewed myself, and I liked others who took that approach. Working hard was one of my values, but I wasn't sure those were the right words. Just 'hard work' seemed to lack something for me. Aside from those two, I had it down to about 30 other options. This was harder than I thought it was going to be. I needed more help.

One of my football coach buddies had texted me last year asking a simple question: "Three words to describe me. Go." It would've been an odd question from most people, but Sam was always doing things like that. "Driven, relentless, and loyal" was my response. Of course, at the time, I didn't ask him to reciprocate—probably because I didn't really want to know the answers.

I had forgotten about it until I started thinking about what I value. Well, not only what I say I value, but what my actions *say* I value. That was the beauty of Sam's question: it gave me immediate feedback on how others viewed me.

But was I really ready to open myself up to this type of feedback? I was definitely nervous and a little scared to hear what people might say. I was finding this growth was beginning to push me out of my comfort zone. I was committed to changing who I was as a West Lake coach and Dax and Rachel's father, though. So I leaned into the discomfort, trusted my courage telling me to go for it, and asked.

I started with those closest to me, of course, but I also asked my assistant coaches, former players, co-workers, and friends. The initial response, especially from my close friends, was "What's wrong with you? Why are you asking this, Mick?" They thought I had gone crazy, which at first I thought was funny, until I realized how much that said about my unwillingness to be vulnerable and seek growth.

Their responses gave me great feedback and some definite direction to finding my core values. *Committed, extra work, dedicated, above expectations, passionate, overachiever, out-work others,* were all replies I received.

Passionate resonated with me because I loved that word and the feeling it gave me. It resolved my difficulty finding the right words for "hard work." For me, passion was more than hard work. It meant going above and beyond, willingly doing extra work others would not. Passionate people walk, talk, and act differently than the average person. I felt like passion described who I was at my best and who I wanted to be.

Overachiever pushed me towards another of my core values, *Tough*. It called on my "inner Rocky." The unrelenting positive mentality and confidence spoke to exactly the person I wanted to be. I had never been the favorite, and I was pretty good with it. I didn't even want it. Nonetheless, the confidence in my ability to accomplish whatever I set out to do never waivered.

Lette was significant in my self-discovery process, too. She had completed a workshop on discovering your *why* as an educator about five years before, and recalled something she thought might help me. The workshop called it Level 5 Moments, borrowed from Simon Sinek's book *Start with Why*. Essentially, you reflect on your life and identify the memorable moments: things that stand out to you as significant even now. You write them down and describe why they are still significant to you, and then you share them with someone. This is where Lette felt the workshop setting fell apart. The people at the workshop didn't know each other well enough to help the other person. She felt the reluctance to be vulnerable blocked the trust needed to get help.

Knowing each other wasn't an issue for Lette and I. We had been together, either married or dating, for almost 15 years. Our relationship survived attending college in different cities, parents telling us we would never make it, bare cupboards and refrigerators, and me coaching basketball. No one knew me better than she did. Lette helped me find two of my core values: Unified and Thankful.

Lette listened as I shared my memorable moments. Some she had never heard before, and some she had probably heard too many times. I shared the most personal stories I had: old high school and college memories from basketball and baseball, those Sunday afternoon football games with my brother, learning about how poor Dad had been growing up, getting smacked in the mouth by Mom for laughing at a kid, my horse dying when I was ten, and finding out about my grandma's heart attack while doing chores at Lette's house. I was as open as I had ever been at any point in my life. It felt good to share stories that impacted me so much, but it was still scary, even sharing them with someone I knew wouldn't judge me for them.

Having the courage to share the stories provided the foundation for the discovery of my values, but Lette's observations and questions were what led to the results. She asked probing questions to get to my heart, and when I showed emotion around a story, she noticed. When she found those, she really dug deep. One of those was getting smacked in the mouth by Mom.

"Why do you remember getting smacked in the mouth by your Mom? I know that wasn't the only time it happened," Lette asked, adding a little jab of humor.

"Ha, it definitely wasn't the only time it happened, but it's the one I remember clearly. I could take you back to the exact spot it happened, all this time later. We were at the county fair and I was maybe nine years old. I was walking with Mom on one side of me and Dad on the other. Ahead of us was a boy about my age with his older brother. Both of them were wearing torn jeans, dirty, oversized shirts, and worn-out shoes with holes in them. I remember pointing at them, laughing, and saying "Look at..." but before I could finish my sentence, Mom busted me square in my mouth," I told Lette.

"But what made it something you still remember? Did it embarrass you?" she replied.

"Well, yeah, I was embarrassed, but it wasn't really that. It was what she said that stuck with me," I said. "She didn't say anything about it until we were finished at the fair and in the car ready to head home. Then she said, "Don't you ever laugh at someone for something they don't have. You don't know what those boys have to go through every day. You just be thankful for what you have. Every day, you should be thankful for what you have. That was your dad growing up. You just laughed and pointed at your dad, Mick.""

When she finished, I dropped my head and looked over at Dad. He never took his eyes off the road, but I can still feel the disappointment he must've felt at the time.

Reflecting on that moment, I told Lette, "That killed me at the time. I was nine and my dad was my hero. It hurt, but it also changed my life. I never did that again, and making fun of someone for having less than you is the surest way to get me fired up to this day. I always want to be thankful for what I have and the opportunities I've been blessed with. I'm much more empathetic with those that are struggling. I don't judge them or think I'm better or they're worse. If I'm in a position to help, I want to help. I realize it's hardly ever a conscious choice to be in those situations."

My head was down when I finished talking, and there was a tear running down my cheek. When I looked up, Lette was smiling and her eyes were welling up.

"It looks like being thankful might be one of your core values," she said.

The other story Lette dug into centered on my view of teamwork as a high school and college basketball player. "I know you loved playing basketball," she began, "but what about it did you like so much?"

"Well, my teammates... that family feeling of counting on another guy and them counting on you. That's what I miss the most," I said.

"What teammates did you like best? she asked. "Not names necessarily, but describe them—what were they like?"

My eyes lit up, which Lette took note of. "I love playing with guys who care about each other and aren't afraid to say it. I've been so lucky to play with so many great teammates. Guys that valued our time together, took advantage of every second together, and would tell you what you can do better with no hint of personal blame. They cared about the team and the results of the team first. I loved playing with those types of guys! That teamwork, that unity, is a part of who I am now," I said.

"Based on the energy you had talking about your teammate now, and in all the other stories I've endured," she said with a wink, "I'm pretty sure something about teamwork or unity should be a core value for you."

CHAPTER EIGHT

REVISITING MY PURPOSE

"Life shrinks or expands in proportion to one's courage."
–Anais Nin

I was gaining some traction with my core values. Now it was time to run them by someone who could give me some honest feedback, so off I went to see Dad again.

"OK. Here's what I've got: Passionate, Unified, Tough, and Thankful. Those are my core values. What do you think?" I asked, eager for his response.

"I like them. That sounds like you. I don't know if it encompasses the fight and grit I see in you, but they're a good start. I love that you're searching for your core values, but you need to make sure you have the big picture in mind," he replied.

The big picture? Having core values and using them to live my life and coach my basketball team wasn't a big enough picture?

"Your *why*—the reason you do what you do, Mick. Remember me telling you about this the last time you were here? You have to have a purpose. If you don't have one, someone else will make one for you—or worse yet, you won't have one. Wouldn't you rather be intentional about the impact you leave? Too many people are indifferent about their life and don't have the courage to stand up and say what's important to them.

"Listen, here's another story for you. Not sure if it's as good as the starfish story, but it's close," he continued.

A young boy was walking along a road when he came across three stonecutters cutting stone for a large building they were constructing. Curious, the boy stopped by the first stonecutter and asked him what he was doing. The first stonecutter slowly looked up, clearly annoyed by the boy, and said, "What's it look like I'm doing? Cutting up this stupid rock. I can't wait until it's time to go home for the day. This is the worst job in the world." The boy looked around and noticed the man's dirty tools were all over the ground and he had made very little progress on the stone he was cutting for the day.

Shrugging it off, the boy continued down the road until he came to a second stonecutter. Again, the boy stopped to ask what he was doing. The second stonecutter, slightly more interested in talking, replied, "I'm just doing my job. I have to cut these stones for this wall I'm building. It pays the bills and gets me to the weekend."

The second stonecutter's tools were laying around his toolbox, but were clearly old and worn.

The boy nodded his head and set out again. When he reached the third stonecutter, the boy stopped and asked what he was doing, just as he had with the previous two. Smiling and grabbing the boy by his shoulders, the stonecutter sat the boy down and began, "Ah, let me tell you!" the third stonecutter said, "I am building a cathedral! I get to craft the stone that goes into every wall of this wonderful building that my kids and my grandkids will enjoy for the rest of their lives. What an honor it is to be a part of this construction." The boy couldn't help but smile as he noticed that all of the third stonecutter's tools were shiny and neatly placed in his toolbox.

After the story, Dad said, "Your purpose determines which stonecutter you are. The world is full of the first two stonecutters. In every walk of life, from garbage man to CEO, you will find far more stonecutters living like them. And thank the Lord, no matter what area of life you explore, you will also find a few like the third stonecutter. When you just settle for doing your job and making a living, you fail to realize that we all have a choice in our profession, our families, or any other part of our life. Your purpose is that choice: do your job, or build a cathedral? It's at the center of everything you do. Your core values are very important, but they just lay out how you will go about fulfilling your purpose."

"Dad, I thought helping people understand my core values was my purpose. Now you're telling me that my core values aren't the same as my purpose," I told him.

"You're not that far away. You've done all this self-reflection and self-discovery. You're close to your purpose. I think I know your *why*," he replied.

Of course, it would be too easy for him to just tell me, so he continued down his path of questioning.

"Let's go back to this underdog thing you mentioned when talking about playing football with your brother. What makes you like the underdog role so much? Why Rocky? I mean, Rocky loses in *Rocky I* and *Rocky III*. Why do you like that so much?" Dad asked.

"It has nothing to do with him winning. It's the courage to try, knowing you might fail. It's the pursuit of being as good as you can possibly be. Rocky wasn't the most talented, most gifted, biggest, strongest, but he gave everything he had. He was the best he could be with what he had. That's what I love about the Rocky movies," I told him.

"OK. I get that. But the underdog doesn't always win. As a matter of fact, he usually doesn't win. How is it ok to not win, to not succeed? Are you saying as long as you try your best, that's good enough? We're all winners?" Dad probed, with clear sarcasm in his final question.

Dad knew he was pushing serious buttons now, but I didn't.

He continued, "What do you mean by *succeed*? So you're telling me the kid that comes to the gym on his own at 6:00 am every morning, puts in extra work in the weightroom, and scratches and claws in practice just to make the team is less successful than the kid that doesn't do any of that and is a starter? Come on. That's not right. The kid with limited athletic ability who outworks everyone and the super-gifted athletic freak—are those two equal? No way. I don't believe that. Society wants to box you in and define success for you, telling you the score doesn't lie, your salary is your worth. I don't like that and I don't believe it's true."

"Dad, you know I agree with you. Society's definition of success is jacked up. If I grew up to be a doctor or a lawyer, society would immediately deem me successful. But what if deep down I really wanted to be an artist or a teacher? Then am I really a success? I don't think so. Then I'm basing success on what other people are telling me, not on what I truly believe. I don't want to do that," I said.

"That's exactly what you've been doing," he replied.

"Well, I'm not doing it anymore," I snapped back at him.

"Glad to hear it. You're almost there. Think about it. Write it down. Figure out your purpose, and your core values will fall right into place. You'll feel it when it's right," he said.

I thanked Dad for helping me again, and headed home. I was anxious to drive because that's where I do some of my best thinking.

All of the discussions from the past few weeks were running through my head. The starfish, the stonecutters, the Level 5 moments... all the truth serum from the people around me. I knew Dad's rant had just hit a nerve. The underdog thing was important to me, but I didn't think that was it. I loved overachievers, but something was missing. Success. What is success? It really isn't what people say it is. I know so many people that make a lot of money or win a lot of games, but either don't do it the right way or aren't happy. Is that really success? I don't think success is what I'm after. It's more than that. The questions were eating at my soul, but I soaked in them.

Two days later, while mowing the yard, it came to me.

It was about excellence, not success. *Excellence* was the word that had been escaping me. *Excellence* was what mattered to me. I had to call Dad to let him know.

"I've got it, Dad! Excellence over success. I want to help people strive for excellence over success. Excellence is the best you are capable of becoming. It's following your heart and being the best you can be, wherever that leads you. Success is society's definition of success—money, fame, status, winning. I want to help people understand the difference and empower them to pursue excellence over success," I told him.

I felt like I was floating.

He replied: "That sounds great. I love it. Congratulations! I can't wait to see where this takes you."

CHAPTER NINE

LIVING OUR VALUES OUT LOUD: CRITICAL BEHAVIORS

"Always remember, your focus determines your reality."
–Qui-Gon Jinn in The Phantom Menace, *written by George Lucas*

I spent the next two months brainstorming ways to run the basketball program through the lens of focusing on excellence over success. How to practice, how to play, how to run youth camps—I looked at every facet of our program. With my purpose in place—excellence—it became all about the core values. After all the conversations and time spent thinking, I had settled on four core values: Toughness, Passion, Unity, and Gratitude. Now the question was, what would I *do* with those values besides make signs and hang them on the walls?

These values were my way of living my purpose. If I could help our players become Tough, Passionate, Unified, and Thankful, I would be leading them to value excellence over success—

something I consider a vital life skill as well as my personal purpose.

While I was incredibly excited and empowered by this enlightened approach, I also had an uneasy feeling... mainly because I had no idea how to actually do it. Fortunately for me, the courage to try new ideas was something I had grown to embrace.

A lunch at a local diner with my buddy Sam turned out to add some direction and clarity on exactly how to implement my values, although I don't believe either of us set out with that intention.

Sam was coming to town for a coaching clinic, so we grabbed the opportunity to get together and talk. He was definitely a coach who would roll up his sleeves and work to improve himself and his program.

Sam had been a standout football and basketball player throughout high school, and had gone on to be a successful quarterback at a small college. Being eight years older, I had actually coached against Sam as a player in my first two years as a head coach. He presented himself as brash and arrogant on the field and court, but there was no debating his willingness to compete and the respect he commanded from his teammates. Following his playing days, Sam returned to his alma mater to teach and coach. He immediately jumped in with both feet, serving as freshman basketball coach and assistant varsity football coach. He quickly progressed up the ranks, landing the head coaching position at his old high school at the age of 23.

Sam attributes his success to luck—being in the right place at the right time—but it was much more a result of his unique work ethic and willingness to learn that propelled him into a leadership role so quickly. Sam was fortunate to have great coaches throughout his playing career, and he started coaching as an assistant to the best of the bunch, Coach Gates. After a few years under this legendary mentor, Sam had a unique approach to coaching and to life in general. His willingness to stay uncomfortable, constantly learning and questioning, sky-rocketed his development. And he was honest—sometimes brutally honest. That brash arrogance he had as a player had turned into an unshakeable confidence and conviction in doing things the right way as a coach.

He was just the guy I needed to talk to.

I started off by sharing my core values and telling him my newly-found purpose. He liked them, but seemed more intrigued than approving. Sam immediately began quizzing me about where my core values came from, why I picked those particular ones, and how I knew they were right. He had a contrarian way about him, constantly challenging your position.

Only after explaining and defending your perspective would Sam relent. Often he would share the same belief I would share with him at the beginning of a conversation, but I wouldn't know it until the end. This was a great test for me at the time, because it reinforced all the reflection and thought I had put into my core values.

Once he had finished barraging me with questions, he finally nodded his head and said, "Those are good. They sound like you."

That was about the most praise you'd get from Sam. He was always more interested in looking forward instead of back, and forward we went. His next set of questions pushed us into a two-hour chase for clarity.

"Now, how do you know if a guy is being tough?" he asked.

At first I thought he was being his normal contrarian self, until I realized he was genuinely asking.

"No really, what do they look like? What does tough look like?" Sam reiterated.

"Tough. You know, play really hard, dive on the floor, get loose balls, practice hard, don't back down... those are the physical things. Mentally, stay focused, be ready to play, stay positive with yourself and your teammates. It means a lot of things," I said as I delved deeper into the discussion.

Sam was pulling out napkins out of the container now. He was clearly enjoying our exploration of this new territory.

"Yeah, I don't know. I think we need to define it. Make it clear to players that when you say *Tough*, this is exactly what it means. How cool would it be if you could zero them in on the one aspect of toughness that ensures it in all other areas of their lives—or at least makes toughness way more likely? The root of toughness," he responded.

"That would be awesome. And if we could get it to a single action, then we could measure it: yes, you were Tough; no, you weren't. So what is Tough?" Sam was jotting down thoughts on the napkins, so I kept going with the questions.

"Who do we know that is Tough? What do they consistently do? We know it's more than physical. There are plenty of players and people who appear physically tough, but are only putting on a front. When they hit trouble or adversity, they crumble. And we know it's more than mental; there is a physical component to it, especially in football and basketball," I said to Sam.

"True. Yeah, but the mental is more important, don't you think?" Sam was thinking out loud now.

"For sure. You can't be truly physically tough without being mentally tough. David Goggins is the toughest guy I've read about. He's a physical specimen, but the mentality that he has and his approach to failure and adversity are what makes him elite. Goggins broke the world record for pull-ups in 24 hours. The record is 4,025 pull-ups. Do you know how many he had to do to break the record? Not 4,026—try over 10,450. He failed twice in his attempt. The mentality to not waiver, to come back and go at it again and again. That's what really makes you Tough, right?"

Sam was talking, writing, clicking his pen, then talking and clicking his pen again... all at the same time now.

"Definitely. I've got grit, persistence, relentless, never quit, never back down, show up, compete, and fighter mentality. You got any others?" he asked.

I added a few, and then we spent the next hour and a half debating the accuracy of each word as truly descriptive of *Tough*. We had napkins spread across the table with notes, arrows, and crossed-out words. It looked like the evidence wall on one of those crime shows. We finally zeroed in on *show up*.

We felt like the toughest people may have all of those other characteristics, but they weren't measurable.

As Sam put it, "I like *relentless*, but how do you measure that? We can tell if someone shows up or not, though. We can tell that every single time. And if you don't show up, you can't be relentless, you can't be Tough. Showing up is at the root of toughness. Tough people show up every time."

It was close, but I felt like *showing up* was missing something too, so I pushed.

"Don't you think *how* they show up is important? I mean, I don't know about you, but we have guys who show up but don't exhibit an ounce of toughness, because they don't look like they want to be there—they're too tired or they're mad about something. They show up, but they actually hurt the overall toughness of the group by the *way* they show up," I said.

Sam thought, stared off to his left, and clicked his pen incessantly.

Then he said, "For sure. How about body language? Positive body language. Tough guys always have positive body language. There are no exceptions to that. Can you think of any? I mean, everyone has lapses now and then. But positive body language is present at every single moment we show Toughness. We can see it immediately when someone walks in the door."

It definitely wasn't the obvious choice, but it was perfect for a root characteristic of Toughness. Toughness is impossible without positive body language. We tried to find an example that didn't fit, and failed. Toughness demands positive body language.

"Simple. I love it. Toughness is positive body language. That's how we define it and that's how we evaluate it. It doesn't matter if it's on the court, in the classroom, or in the locker room. We can always display Toughness through our body language," I said.

What a discussion! We were both energized by the clarity we had discovered, yet humbled by the simplicity we had been missing for so many years. How could we have missed this? As quickly as I thought of posing the question, I moved beyond it.

"Now I need your help on the other three!" I said.

Sam laughed, picked at his food a little, then jumped in on helping me with my other three core values. When we were finished, we had everything sketched out on a single napkin: my core values and the behaviors that bring them to life.

At the root of *Passion* was choosing extra work. We agreed one of the most significant separators of passionate people is their willingness to do extra, to go above and beyond expectations.

People that are passionate about what they do always choose to do extra.

Unified meant to speak and act with urgency. I found one of the biggest challenges for my players was to hold their peers accountable to the standards we agreed on, because they don't want to hurt their feelings or have them hold a grudge. To me, this has always been a form of selfishness. When we choose not to hold a teammate accountable because it's uncomfortable, we choose our comfort over the good of the team. Teams that value every opportunity they have together speak and act with urgency. They don't waste time because they value the group over themselves.

For the core value *Thankful*, showing love was the behavior we came to expect. The expression of gratitude is important, but showing it is another. Too many people fail to share the love they feel for others, leaving it under the table, an unopened present. By sharing gratitude, we become more aware of what we have to be thankful for and show our appreciation of it.

These standards were my core values in action. They were my personal standards and also my contribution to the world—and at that time, our basketball team and my family were my world. I remember feeling so alive and ready for the season to get started.

STANDARDS OF EXCELLENCE	
Core Value	**Critical Behavior**
Tough	Positive body language
Passionate	Choose extra work
Unified	Speak and act with urgency
Thankful	Show love

CHAPTER TEN

COMMITTING TO THE PATH: TRYOUTS

"One life is all we have, and we live it as we believe in living it.
But to sacrifice what you are and to live without belief,
that is a fate more terrible than dying."
–Joan of Arc

I wanted to introduce all of this to our guys in the off-season, but didn't feel like I had it all in place. This was a one-shot deal, and the way it was first presented was going to be really important. So I decided to wait until our first practice to roll out our newly developed Standards of Excellence. It gave me time to get everything organized, and I thought it would be a good to have a fresh, clean start at the beginning of the season. The Standards of Excellence were the nucleus of our changes, but there were plenty of other revisions necessary to raise our program to the level our kids deserved.

The first new element the players were introduced to were Skull Sessions. Players needed to be dressed and ready fifteen minutes before practice was scheduled to begin. I organized Skull Sessions as 15-minute mini-lessons in our core values. Players took notes and engaged in a variety of activities and discussions. We had held similar meetings in the past, but never consistently or to cover specific content. They had typically been used for game-planning or for delivering a wake-up call following a poor performance. I felt the consistency of the meetings would help communicate the significance I was placing on our core values and standards.

Tryouts began with a slightly different message also.

I told them, "OK, guys, I want to thank you all for trying out. Before we get started, I want to share with you the purpose of our basketball program. Then it's your choice if you think this is a program you still want to be a part of. Obviously, we want to win games, and we're going to do everything we can to do that, but we are also seeking a larger purpose, a higher calling. In this program, we are going to pursue personal and team excellence. Excellence is different from success. We are used to them being defined as basically the same thing, but they definitely are not.

"Success, as it's currently defined in our society, is based on comparing ourselves with other people. We want to help you become the best possible version of yourself without basing your worth on how society tells you to measure it. In society, success is money, fame, sex, houses, cars, status, followers. In sports, it's based on winning, starting, highlights, points, clout. We acknowledge those things, but those are not our pursuit in this program.

"We are striving for *excellence*. We want to do the absolute best we can: prepare to the best of our ability, play as hard as possible, work as a team, compete at the highest level. We want to commit ourselves to the process that will get us there, be loyal, faithful, and diligent in that process, and then willingly accept and embrace the outcome. The scoreboard will tell us if we won or lost by society's gauge. Our faithfulness to the process will tell us how close we came to excellence. I know this approach is different than what most results-driven teams pursue. It's not an easy concept to grasp, but that's what we're after."

Surrendering the outcome was important to me. This is really the ultimate goal of not just coaching, but living. The time reflecting and thinking about the insights from all the important people in my life led me to that point. Trusting the process was about being relentless in your preparation, faithful in your relationships, and steadfast in your duties. It was trusting the commitment you had made and the work you had done. It wasn't complacency or entitlement; it was humility and freedom.

I continued, "Surrendering the outcome is the ultimate form of competition. Some people confuse it with the 'as long as you did your best' tag-line. That's not it at all. 'As long as you did your best' is submissive, and robs those believing it of the true power they possess. It's weak and soft. Who doesn't do their best at the moment? No one wants to fail or be embarrassed. But surrendering the outcome is different. It requires putting in effort before the moment. Surrendering the outcome demands meticulous preparation and a full commitment to the task at hand. Surrender is impossible without the prep work. If you haven't prepared and put in the work at an elite level, then you are incapable of surrendering the outcome. You will spend all your time worrying if you're ready, if you can do it, or if you've done enough. You'll spend your energy worrying about a bunch of things you can't control, or you'll eventually just give in to the moment and 'do your best.'

"Surrendering the outcome is either liberating and empowering or it's a scary waste of time. We want it to liberate us. To propel us to the next level of competing, of living. No fears of failure or judgement, just the absolute best we've got, and we will take whatever happens. That's the way to compete. *That's* the way to live," I said. I was pretty fired up.

I paused to make eye contact with each player. Then I continued, "In order to do that, we are going to focus on practicing, playing, and living with four core values. These are going to be the staple of our program. Of course I want you to become better players as a result of being in our program, and I want you to have the opportunity to play in college if you want to, but more than anything I want you to grow in these four areas, because growth in these four areas will ensure that the purpose I just shared with you—excellence— comes to fruition."

"The first value is Toughness. Now, *Tough* can mean a lot of things. For us, Tough is going to mean positive body language. I know—not really the first thing you think of when you hear the word *tough*. But our body language is an outward expression of our attitude. We want that to be strong, positive, and uplifting to those around us. It's important we realize the impact of our body language on the people around us. In meetings, in class, in practice, on the bus, on the floor, on the bench. *Tough*, for us, is positive body language that gives energy to ourselves and those around us.

"The second value is *Passion*. We believe in work, and doing more work than is expected. I don't believe you can ever reach your full potential by just doing the minimum. The thing that sets people apart in terms of their performance is what they do outside of the required time. So, for being *Passionate*, we are talking about choosing extra work.

"Our third value is *Unity*. Clearly, playing together as a team is vital to our success on the floor. One of the key elements of any great teammate I've ever had is a sense of urgency. The most Unified teams always valued the time we had together so much, we refused to waste it. You could see that urgency in how these teammates talked, walked, and worked. So when we talk about being *unified*, we're talking about speaking and acting on point, with urgency.

"The final core value we will focus on is *Gratitude*. I believe there is too much entitlement in the world. Too many people think they are owed something, which leads to this victimhood mentality. We want to fight that. We want to make sure we recognize the good things that happen to us and not take them for granted. We want to make sure our teammates and the people around us know we're grateful for them and what they do for us. Not because it helps us win, which it does, but because it's the right way to live. The way we show we are *Thankful* for each other is showing love."

The room was silent. Most of the guys still had their heads down, writing in their notebooks. Some had their eyebrows raised, and some were nodding in agreement. I really had no idea how it would go from there. This approach was clearly different from the paths I and their previous coaches had taken in the past. It was certainly going to be different. But who says different is bad?

CHAPTER ELEVEN

THE CHALLENGE TO STAND UP FOR VALUES

"A gem cannot be polished without friction,
nor man perfected without trials."
—Confucious

Tryouts are the worst part of coaching. Telling a young player they cannot be a part of a team they have worked so hard to be included on cuts right to your heart. I spent countless hours with most of these guys: open gyms, weight-lifting sessions, group skill trainings, and conditioning workouts. In most cases, we had already established a relationship. The only solace I found in selecting the team revolves around time. We expected a lot from our players and required considerable sacrifice in other areas of their lives. I had always felt it was unfair to aplayer to monopolize his time if he was never going to actually play. This season, I had decided to do something that other coaches had advised me against: keeping someone on the team who will never play.

I talked to each player individually to let them know whether they made the team or not, and what I envisioned their role on the team being that season if they did make it. For those not making the team, I would share things to improve on and recreational league options in the area. Those conversations are hard, but an important opportunity for growth for all involved.

When I came to Kyle, who I had decided to keep on the team, I knew I wanted to take the same approach: be honest, upfront, and straightforward. I began by thanking him for his work in the off-season and for having the courage to try out. Then I told him that I did not see him in the rotation; that he would likely play only in lopsided games that we had a big lead in, but that I did want him to be a part of the team. I shared his unselfishness and willingness to embrace our core values as being the key areas he could bear the standards for this year's team. I finished up by asking Kyle to consider the time commitment and expectations, and then go home and talk to his parents about the proposition before giving me an answer. I told him my proposal wasn't right for everyone, but I thought he could make a great, positive impact on the team. Thankfully for us, Kyle agreed, and became a major contributor to our team while playing very few minutes on the season.

As the team was selected and practices started piling up, we stayed consistent with our Skull Sessions and core value discussions. I felt like guys were starting to understand and embrace them. I did my best to be intentional about referencing them often in practice, as did our assistant coaches.

In one of our Skull Session activities, players rated themselves on how they had been doing with each core value. Then they selected a teammate who best exemplified each core value so far in the season. Highlighting a teammate encouraged those doing a good job to continue down that road. We talked about ways they could improve individually in living each value.

As good as those discussions had been, the reality of playing time always seemed to have a way of dampening the spirits of players on the short end of it. Kids want to play. Coaches want kids that want to play. I could tell we had players unhappy with playing time because they were showing it in practice, which often leads to the parent meetings most coaches dread.

It seemed like meetings with parents always had one focal point: their son's playing time. In the past, I viewed this perspective as selfish and contrary to the objective of a team, mainly because the player's attitude was so often skewed by that of their parents. I struggled to see it any other way. It got old pretty quickly when I had meetings with multiple players about their position on the team. We weren't not even playing real games yet, and players and parents were upset their son was playing JV instead of varsity. To me, this was like me trying to tell a mechanic how to fix a motor. I don't know that profession or all the intricate details of it, nor do I spend time trying to understand it. The same is true for most parents sitting in those meetings.

After five years of enduring brutal parent meetings, I had finally committed to an ideal that would help me and the parent through them: our core values. My first test was with a returning varsity letterman, Carl, who was frustrated to be seeing less playing time than a freshman playing the same position.

Carl was a good player who had played significant minutes in a reserve role for us the previous season as a junior. He clearly thought that he would step right into one of the vacated starting positions since he would be a senior. That wasn't the case, which led to some behavior from Carl that would negatively impact his playing time if not addressed right away. I decided to initiate a meeting with his father, who was the only parent in the picture at the time. His dad was ultra-confident in Carl's abilities and had expressed dissatisfaction with Carl coming off the bench the previous year, a distraction that I chose to ignore, which was clearly a mistake in retrospect. The new me made a conscious choice to not ignore anything that could impact our team—and any type of dissatisfaction that culminates in destructive behavior impacts the team.

I shook hands with Carl and his father at the office door, as did the assistant coach who joined me. Carl sat on the couch, leaned back, and slouched down. His dad sat forward, leaning on his elbows, clearly more interested in the conversation than Carl. I began the meeting by praising Carl's potential, recognizing his talent, and sharing how instrumental he was to the success of our team. Carl's dad nodded in agreement, clearly wondering why his son wasn't playing more or even starting. Carl and his father were clearly in agreement with my initial message. Next, I explained our core values and critical behaviors. I told him helping our players grow in these core values was the ultimate goal of our program.

"Man, come on. Carl is trying to play college basketball. He needs to be on the floor for scouts to see him, and you're sitting here talking about some core values," was his dad's immediate response.

I consciously slowed myself down in order to clearly convey my next message.

"Our core values are to be Tough, to show positive body language. Do you think college coaches want to see players that pout after every mistake, or players that are positive and ready to go, no matter what happens? Our next value is passionate: choosing extra work. Do you think college players have to be willing to put in work outside of regular practice in order to compete at that level? Next is Unified, to speak and act with urgency. Are college players expected to communicate and act like what they're doing matters? Our last value is to be Thankful, to show love. If you were a college coach, would you want a player that embraces and celebrates their teammates, or one that is always going off by himself or looking for attention?"

Silence. Carl's dad glared at Carl, then turned to me and said, "So, you're telling me he isn't doing those things in practice? I see some of it in the game, but nothing other guys don't do too. Carl, you doing this stuff in practice? You getting any work in outside of practice?"

Carl sat up straight now and responded, "I mean, sometimes I'm mad or in a bad mood, and don't feel like having positive body language or talking to my teammates. Most of the time I'm just tired. And when I mess up, I get so mad at myself that I just need to get away from people."

His dad was becoming skeptical now. "And how about putting in some extra work? You working on your game before or after practice at all?" he asked forcefully.

"I mean, sometimes I come in before school, like once a week, maybe," Carl answered, now looking down towards the ground.

I took advantage of the break in dialogue to jump in. I said, "This isn't a meeting to tell you Carl is in trouble or getting suspended or anything like that. More than anything, I wanted to let you know he isn't meeting the standard we expect from the guys on this team. We've shared this with Carl multiple times, so we thought it was important that you were aware also. He's more than capable of meeting the standards—we've seen him do it. The concern is, if he continues down the path he is currently going, his playing time will continue to decrease. We need Carl to embrace our core values, not only for his future as a player, but also for his future as a man."

I added to Carl, "And the gym is open every morning at 6:00 am. If you want to play college ball, I should see you five days a week."

His dad, now seemingly satisfied, stood, shook my hand, and said, "Oh, he'll be there."

When I started viewing meetings as an opportunity to work with parents to help their son, they became much more productive and less stressful. Perspective was the critical piece. That meeting was the first time a parent meeting had actually energized me. Having the courage to stand on our core values had not only given me direction and clarity to share with Carl's dad, but it had empowered me and given me more confidence to build on.

I wish I could say the rest of the early season went that well. Carl's meeting aside, the implementation of our new culture had only been successful in the locker room. The results on the court took longer to materialize.

A few weeks into the regular season, we were struggling to win games. As any coach will tell you, winning solves a lot of problems and losing magnifies them.

Players understanding their roles has always been a challenge in basketball. When done correctly, it makes this sport one of the most poetic events to watch. The game just flows when roles are in order and players embrace them. That's the issue, though—embracing them. It's not enough to just accept them. Accepting is passive, and embracing is aggressive. Players have to lean into their roles, looking for ways to fill them. We were in the accepting mode, looking for ways out of the responsibilities of our roles. And it showed up on the court.

Honestly, it was a mess. All this planning, purpose, and core value development I had committed to wasn't paying off the way I had envisioned it. We talked about the values all the time, but the basketball and team aspect of everything had not changed for all for us. We were just as sloppy, just as undisciplined as we had been in previous years. And, if I was being honest with myself, once we walked in the gym, I was pretty much the same, too. I never thought about or mentioned core values during practices or games. I wasn't really teaching the core values. I was talking about them, but I wasn't teaching them. Core values are verbs: actions. They need to be done, not talked about.

Thankfully, I had a couple of friends who would help me see that clearly in the next few days.

CHAPTER TWELVE

WALKING THE TALK (OR NOT)

"Being honest may not get you a lot of friends,
but it'll always get you the right ones."
–John Lennon

C oach Gale had been an assistant coach for us for several years. He didn't have a ton of coaching experience, unless you count youth soccer, but he had commitment and a willingness to say what he thought. He loved the core value approach that we had taken and was the best we had at using the core values as teaching points during play. He wasn't confrontational, but he understood conviction.

Something was clearly on Coach Gale's mind. As we began our post-practice coaches' meeting, Coach Gale started right in.

"Who are we? As a team, what is our identity? I'm asking because I don't know. We're almost halfway through the season, and I don't know who we are. And if I don't know, I really doubt if any of the guys in the locker room know," he said.

I immediately flashed back to the conversation with my dad, when he pointed out that my core values were different from my purpose. The core values simply laid the path to fulfilling my purpose, but this was my identity. Living my core values was my process. It made me, me. Our team needed to understand that our identity rests on in living the core values. That would create the identity of our team, but we have to do it. Consistently.

"Good question, Coach. I don't know, " I replied. "We don't have one right now. I want us to be Tough, Passionate, Unified, and Thankful. That's what I want our identity to be, but that's not who we are right now."

Coach Gale jumped in.

"Mick, we're not even close to that. Tough is positive body language, and we have guys late to practice or not dressed and ready on time. How can you have positive body language if you're not even here? Passionate? Choosing extra work? Three of our starters never get extra shots or work in. Unified—just watch our bench during a game, and it's clear the two or three guys who aren't unified. For Thankful, all you have to do is walk in the locker room—the place is a mess. Guys leave trash on the floor, don't clean up after themselves, shut the door so JV and freshman guys can't come in.

"Coach, it's exactly who we were last year. I love the core values and what they stand for, but we aren't following through on them. My concern is that our guys are going to dismiss them as just another thing we do. If they do that, Coach, we are missing a huge opportunity to change their lives," he said.

I was a little surprised by how open I was to his criticism. I didn't want to hear it, but he was right. Rather than discourage me, his feedback invigorated me. We had to make the core values real. I spent the rest of that night thinking about actions. What could we do to live these values in our basketball program? Thanks to Coach Gale's willingness to be honest, I had some great thoughts and notes to work from going forward.

If Coach Gale's words had been critical, the next day of practice would be brutal. One of my ideas prior to the season was to invite other coaches in to evaluate our practice. They would give feedback on how they thought practice was being run and, more importantly, how we were doing with our core values. One of the questions I wanted to be answered was "What do you think we value?"

I felt like if we were teaching our core values properly, something about those values should surface with any observation. The coaches who had been in earlier in the season had given some good feedback, but nothing really tangible or critical enough to help us. For the most part, their observations had been generic. "Your kids play hard." "They seem coachable." "They really compete in practice."

Sam was scheduled to observe this practice, so I knew one thing: I was going to get honest, critical feedback. Based on my conversation with Coach Gale, it wasn't going to be too positive, either, but I was ok with that. I remember thinking the basketball gods must've been looking out for me to send both messages so close together. They were saying "Dude, we can't tell you any more clearly, get this right!"

Sam was there 30 minutes before practice, clipboard and pen in hand. During practice, he mingled through drills, stuck his head into huddles, asked assistant coaches questions, and stood close enough to players to hear what they had to say to each other. He was fully engaged in the practice, not simply observing it. After practice, we sat down in the coaches' office. He didn't wait for me to ask any questions.

He said, "What was *that*? Bro, that was awful. The basketball was bad and the culture is worse. You talked about a bunch of stuff in your Skull Session that didn't carry over one bit to that practice. You have all these signs and sayings on the wall, but they don't mean anything to those guys. Your body language is negative or neutral, and your players' body language is just as bad most of the time. Maybe there are two kids who have positive body language consistently—but there is no urgency.

Guys run from one drill to another because you're yelling at them, not because they think it's important. If guys aren't in a drill, they are disengaged. They're never outside the drill watching, asking questions, or encouraging their teammates. And showing love? Those guys think toughness is talking trash to each other and trying to humiliate a teammate, like it's a rank system or pecking order."

Sam had a gift for directness. He took a breath to reload for his final thoughts.

"It's easy, Mick. Decide who you want to be. It's on you. Your team is a reflection of you, not of them. We talked about all those core values and actions. That's great stuff. But it's only great stuff if it translates to them. It's not about your feelings. You can't decide you want to coach with those values because it makes you feel better about coaching. You have to choose to coach with those values because the position you are in comes with a huge responsibility and your guys are counting on you. They're counting on you to help them become men. They're counting on you to teach them what the world is about.

"What you are trying to do is awesome. You will change the lives of so many kids doing it that way, but those guys in your huddle have to be the center of your purpose. You're too worried about winning or losing games or what people are saying about you. Forget that. Commit to who you want to be as a coach, and then have the guts to go be it. What is it you say you want your guys to do? Surrender the outcome? Do that. Right now they, and you, aren't surrendering anything. You're trying to control an outcome that can't be controlled. Focus on the process. That's how you surrender the outcome."

Initially, I put the walls up in my mind and started to defend against everything Sam had just attacked, with mental justifications for each point. But as I sat there staring at the white board in my office, my defensiveness went from embarrassment to frustration to determination. That was enough wake-up calls for me. The basketball gods had done their part; it was time for me to do mine. He was exactly right. We had been talking a good game, but the execution and follow-through wasn't where it needed to be. This wasn't our guys' fault—it was mine. Honestly, I knew we were missing the mark. Our culture was better, but not where the program was capable of going, and not where I envisioned it.

I wanted to point at things outside of myself that were holding us back again. But now, with full belief in my core values, I was prepared to fight for it. Before I could help our guys, though, I had to help myself.

CHAPTER THIRTEEN

FINDING MY MANTRA

"Quiet the mind and the soul will speak."

–Ma Jaya Sati

I had to get myself right before I could help our players. I had been on the right track, but as soon as the pressure of games hit, I went right back to my comfort zone. That had to change, and the first thing I needed to do was to adjust my relationship with failure. A few years ago, I had watched a Kobe Bryant video at Brett Ledbetter's website, What Drives Winning, in which Kobe talks about the entire concept of failure being a myth, something that doesn't exist. We only allow it to exist when we quit. All the other times, it's simply a learning experience that has made us better. I loved that perspective, but was terrible at embracing it.

I began asking myself,"How did Kobe do that? How did he not sink back to comfort?" I came to a simple but profound answer. He didn't care what other people thought about him. He detached himself from the approval of others. Not needing the approval of others, he was free to fail, learn, grow, fail, learn, grow, and so the process continued.

That brought me to the next question: how did he get to that mindset of not seeking the approval of others, especially in times of adversity, when everyone else reverts to safety and comfort? That answer seemed pretty easy, because it had to be his confidence. Confidence in himself, confidence in his faith. Whatever it was, he had a belief that allowed him to be an unbiased observer of his life, not the controller of it.

I needed to find the source of that confidence for me. I loved my purpose and my core values. They gave me energy, but when things got tough, I needed a reset button for my focus and my emotions—something that took me from the views of the world and brought me back to my beliefs. I needed a mantra.

Right away, I thought of a scene from the movie *Secretariat* that always stirred emotion in me. In the final race scene, when the horse comes around the final turn, everything goes quiet except for the sound of his breathing and his hooves hitting the ground. Everything slows down, and Secretariat's owner reads an adaptation of Job 39:19.

> *"Do you give the horse his strength or clothe his neck with a flowing mane? Do you make him leap like a locust, striking terror with his*

loud snorting? He paws fiercely, rejoicing in his strength, and charges into the fray. He laughs at fear, afraid of nothing, he does not shy away from the sword. The quiver rattles against his side, along with the flashing spear and lance. In frenzied excitement he eats up the ground; he cannot stand still when the trumpet sounds."

That quote reminded me of the purity of competition, the careless freedom required to give everything within with no consideration of loss or judgement. The more I ran the quote through my mind, the more it resonated. Within 20 minutes, I had filtered it down to a version that fit me.

"I laugh at fear, afraid of nothing. I will not shy away from the sword. I will not stand still when the trumpet sounds."

Each sentence spoke to a different part of me.

"I laugh at fear, afraid of nothing" was my reminder that I wasn't in control. I trusted my life to something bigger and more powerful than me. What was there to be afraid of? Someone not agreeing with me? Failing in a basketball game? It all became so trivial from that perspective.

"I will not shy away from the sword" was a reminder to stay in the complexity growth ring as much as possible. In Bill Eckstrom's TED Talk, "Why Comfort Will Ruin Your Life", he talks about growth rings. They are Stagnation, Order, Complexity, and Chaos. Nothing really happens in Stagnation or Chaos because they are too extreme on both ends of the spectrum. Most people do everything they can to stay in Order, because that's comfortable and safe. The problem is, that's not where we grow and improve. That happens only in Complexity. Do not shy away from the sword: take risks, go against the crowd, say what needs to be said.

"I will not stand still when the trumpet sounds" means that when it was time to go, I was going to be ready, and I wasn't going to flinch. I was determined to just do my best and let go with no worries. I was committed to surrendering the outcome and living with no concerns of others' judgment.

The mantra, or reset button, seemed like a little thing that shouldn't make that much difference, but it was powerful because it returned me to my desired mindset. I just needed to train myself to repeat it whenever I felt myself drifting away.

CHAPTER FOURTEEN

THE REAL MICK SHOWS UP

"Actions express priority."
–Gandhi

B ack in front of the team at our next practice's Skull Session, I finally did what I needed to do from the start. I let them see the real me. My fears, my struggles, it was all out in front of them. I had spent way too much time trying to appear strong ignoring, or hiding, his own weaknesses. The reality was I had far more weaknesses than strengths, and trying to deny or hide them didn't make them go away. I was pursuing excellence, but I was learning and trying to do my best, just like them.

"OK, guys. First, I want to apologize for not following through the way I need to on the core values that we've been talking about in Skull. We haven't done a very good job of coaching you guys through these values. We talk about them in here, but this is where we've been leaving them. We're going to do a better job of helping you connect to the core values on the basketball court. They're important. These values are what will change your life, not the basketball.

"And I want you to know you're going to get the best me I have. Up to this point in my coaching career, I've tried to be someone I'm not. I've tried to fit into this coach's mold that I thought I was supposed to be. I wanted to be this all-knowing, macho guy, but really, there's a ton of stuff I don't know. And I'm not macho, I'm average in just about every possible way you can be," I said to the group.

I paused to gather my thoughts, knowing they were taking everything in by how much they were leaning forward and giving me eye contact.

I continued, "But I love you guys. I want to help you become the best sons, friends, husbands, fathers, brothers, teammates, and basketball players you can possibly be. I think that happens through our core values. I believe the basketball that we play on the floor is important, but will be limited by our belief and buy-in to those core values. Every team in the state sets out to win the State Championship, as they should. But we approach things differently. We're going to focus solely on the process it takes to be our very best basketball players and people. If we trust the process, we're going to look up at the end of the season and be a pretty good basketball team. Maybe that's good enough to win a State Championship and maybe it's not, but we're going to honor the process and not worry about the outcome. We want to play our best game last. I think we can all live with that. I know I can."

The locker room had a quiet focus to it. In that moment, players began seeing the bigger picture. They were more open to coaching because of the connection to them as a person, not just them as a basketball player. They were more intentional about developing relationships because they could now see the impact it had on their life, not just the team. And they were more honest with each other about their strengths and weaknesses because they understood their part in helping a teammate become their personal best.

From that point on, our practices were different. Coaches were more engaged and intentional with connecting our core values to basketball. Jogging back on defense was no longer *lazy*, it was *not being Unified*. Throwing your hands up like you were fouled in a drill was no longer ignored by coaches; it was bad body language and a violation of our core value *Tough*. Players outside of drills were no longer quiet observers; they were talking, encouraging, or correcting, or else it lacked the urgency that being unified required. We were also sure to show love to each other following practice by allowing guys a few minutes to get touches in with teammates, whether that be a dap or a hug. You could physically feel the difference in energy.

Our Skull Sessions became much better also. In one of the more powerful ones, we brainstormed the strong and weak voices that we say to ourselves. Most guys were surprised they weren't the only ones with all those weak voices running through their head. From that, we had each guy pick or create their own mantra, or go-to strong voice.

We helped our players create their own failure recovery system, too. I showed a video of Sue Enquist, former UCLA softball coach, talking about what her team did following a mistake. Her players had to pat their chest, call the number of outs, and point at a teammate. We identified the three key aspects of the system: own it, get present, move on. Then our guys created a failure recovery system for themselves involving their mantra, and one for our team following a turnover or mistake. Our team would pat their chest and say "my bad," get a touch from each teammate on the floor, and call out the player on the other team they are responsible for.

We talked about the best ways to show love to each other. I shared some of my takeaways from Gary Chapman's book *The Five Love Languages*, and then we created a document showing the best three ways to show each player on the team love. That Skull Session was impactful for our guys because most had never thought about how they processed affection or how they could best express it to another person. It had a significant impact on how thankful our guys were.

Of course we also talked about basketball, but our focus was on building trust and improving our core values.

The team had turned a corner, but more than anything, I noticed how different I felt compared to the previous year, or even earlier in the season. Very little of it had to do with the results of the games. Our players and coaches were doing such a great job of embracing our values, being vulnerable with each other, and focusing on the process that practice was the highlight of my day.

CHAPTER FIFTEEN

ADDING OUR BELIEFS

*"Mountains are the means; man is the end.
The goal is not to reach the top of the mountains,
but to improve the man."*
–Aron Ralston

I was finally realizing what I had thought but only said occasionally was actually true. Our core values and the things we did in the locker room really *were* more important than the basketball.

I had been saying that for a few years, but it was just 'coach speak'. It sounded good, like I was being noble, but I was finding out when I truly focused on how we could build our players as people, equip them to deal with adversity, and trust each other, rather than only talk about it, it worked. We could live by core values when things were good, when things were bad, when we thought we had time, and when we didn't think we had time. It was a simple choice.

Faithfulness in little things has a way of working itself into big things. Our consistent focus over weeks and months impacted our coaches as much as our players. This complete submersion into our core values led to one of the best additions to how we communicated our values to our players, and it was initiated completely by an assistant coach.

Ethan—E for short—had been coaching with me for 12 years. He was the epitome of a servant leader. Up until this point, he rarely disagreed with me or offered his true opinions and thoughts. He worked like crazy and was unwavering in his loyalty and belief in me and our program. He loved everything about what we did.

Following a Saturday morning practice, E brought me a concern he had about our core values. He wasted no time getting to his point. "I think we need to do something about the core values, Mick."

It caught me a little off guard, especially with how well things had been going.

"What do you have in mind? Do we need to change one or teach it differently?" I said, intrigued to hear his ideas.

He said, "No, no. It's not that. The values and behaviors are great. You know I love them. I just think we need something that paints a more clear picture for guys with what we mean by each one. 'Be Tough, have positive body language' says exactly what we want it to say, but it's just kind of ... I don't know, clunky to say over and over in practice. I think a short little tagline that shares your belief of what that value really looks like would help.

"For example, when we're talking about toughness and body language, I always think of a fighter coming into the ring. He's got a singular focus, he's fully committed, he walks with confidence. He's 'Fight Ready'. For me, 'Fight Ready' conveys everything we've talked about for Toughness. It paints a picture in the minds of our players that other words and phrases just can't do."

I was blown away. What an awesome addition to how we teach our guys and relay what we believe.

Our coaches spent the next two days hashing through potential "beliefs," as we called them, and adding them to the chart. The best part was, none of them came from me. I was in the meetings and shared my thoughts, but the beliefs we settled on all originated from one of our assistants. The sad part was, I had wasted so many years stuck on winning basketball games that I had not only been cheating the players out of incredible learning opportunities, but I had also been missing out on allowing our assistant coaches to grow and contribute fully to our program.

Besides Fight Ready, we added catchphrases to illustrate each of the other values.

Passion. Coach Drew was a minor league pitcher prior to joining our staff three years earlier. He was never short on stories, but one struck a chord with our staff in regards to our core values. As Coach Drew recounted, his pitching coach for the Long Island Road Hens was fanatical about trying to expand the strike zone as a pitcher. They worked daily on throwing pitches just on the edge of the strike zone. According to his coach, by working the edges of the plate, the pitcher would get strike calls that were actually outside the zone in later innings. He called it "stealing inches.". We loved the phrase "stealing inches" and decided to use it to our program as part of being Passionate. Stealing Inches could be an extra sprint, running between stations, or being the first team ready to go for the next drill. Stealing Inches is simply looking for opportunities to improve while others rest.

Unified. This only required us to look at some of the things we had been talking about already. Coach E pointed out that when I encouraged players to hold each other accountable, I would often say "don't flinch." For me, Don't Flinch meant to say what needed to be said or do what needed to be done, but avoid modifying your words and actions for the sake of feelings and harmony. Don't Flinch also meant to not let mistakes derail you.

Get up, dust yourself off, and go again. I loved it, as did our other coaches. We were taking something that we had been saying for years and giving it legitimate meaning for our players.

Thankful. This discussion centered on an article I had read called "Winning Touch: Teams That Touch the Most Win the Most, Study Says" by Ben Forer. It had been a while since I had read the article, but I remembered it striking me as a form of gratitude shared from one player to another. The article said that small physical gestures, such as high fives or pats on the back, were huge indicators of successful teams. Coach Brooks connected it to Thankful for us. His position was that each one of those touches said, "We're in this together, I appreciate you, we can do this, and I'm glad you're here." We began to see it's much more important than just a high five. It created belonging, safety, appreciation, and gratitude.

Once we had the beliefs identified, we spent the next Skull rolling them out to the team. The players loved them. They immediately became a part of our team language.

STANDARDS OF EXCELLENCE		
Belief	Critical Behavior	Core Value
Fight Ready	Positive body language	Toughness
Steal Inches	Choose extra work	Passion
Don't Flinch	Speak and act with urgency	Unified
Touches	Show love	Gratitude

CHAPTER SIXTEEN

SAM'S RETURN

"Confidence is courage in action."
–Naomi Saelens

The second half of our regular season went well on and off the court. Our energy and camaraderie was at an all-time high, and it showed in the results. Funny how that works, eh? We reeled off ten straight wins and locked up our conference championship with a few games left to play. The most satisfying part of this accomplishment is that we never discussed it, never set it as a goal, and never compared ourselves to other teams. The team had placed their focus on the process, not the result. They were starting to embrace the fact that result is simply a byproduct of whatever process we choose to follow.

We were just getting ready to wrap up the regular season when Sam was scheduled to come evaluate practice again. If you recall, his last evaluation wasn't so positive, but it was a catalyst for change that I was grateful for.

I remember Sam's second practice evaluation vividly.

We started with Skull, 15 minutes before the scheduled start of practice, as we had all season. All of our players were sitting on stools in front of their lockers, laughing and talking, ready for practice well before the coaches walked in. We started off with a new activity: a daily Thankful journal. I gave them two prompts for their journal to share with the team, and they each took a couple of minutes to write their responses.

1. Two things about their Accountability Partner they were thankful for: things they do that make our team better. A few weeks prior, we had assigned each player a partner they were responsible for and accountable to. This person serves as their 'go-to guy' throughout the year. They used each other for accountability, support, and courage. I was very intentional about choosing partners to deepen relationships that would benefit each individual and the team. The AP relationships had been a great addition and very impactful.

2. One personal weakness someone helped them see that they had improved on.

I gave the group three minutes to write in their journal, and then we went around sharing the answers from all 12 guys in the room, including all of our coaches. The responses were revealing of how far we had come as a team. We laughed a lot and even cried a little. Our players' answers were honest, open, and vulnerable—a far cry from the start of the season.

The only other thing I shared with our guys that day during the Skull Session was a poem titled "Two Kinds of People," by Ella Wheeler Wilcox. In short, the poem says there are two types of people—lifters and leaners. Lifters make life easier for those around them, while leaners make it harder. We want lifters. Our guys then set one goal for how they would lift their AP during the upcoming practice.

As important as our Skull Session discussion was, none of it was why I remember this practice so much. Our first drill when we came out of the locker room burned it into my memory forever.

We had our guys split into two teams of six, as usual. After their initial two laps around the court and break at centercourt, I announced our first drill would be Flock Dance. Our guys had no idea what this was, because it wasn't a basketball drill.

Flock Dance was an improvisational activity that was sure to get guys out of their comfort zones. Guys lined up in one big V formation, similar to the iconic formation of geese flying. The point of the V was the leader. He would pick a dance move to repeat for 10-15 seconds, while everyone else in the group did that same dance move. After about 15 seconds, I would yell 'change' and the leader would fall out of the lead role, back into formation, and the next player would step up into the lead role. We did this all the way through the team until everyone had been the leader. It never failed to deliver two things: guys getting out of their comfort zones and lots of laughter.

Coach E had his favorite dance music—MC Hammer's *"U Can't Touch This"* —cued up and ready to go, and they went! Some danced better than others, but they were all-in and didn't hold back, which is exactly what I was hoping for. Nobody pulled out as a move to protect themselves from criticism or hate from teammates. Their willingness to be vulnerable because they felt safe was a huge signal that our team was getting it.

Practice following our dance-off was as sharp and focused as it had been for weeks. Guys were engaged and communicating in and out of drills, andplayers huddled in tight circles with their arms around each other. Guys were constantly giving out high fives and pats on the back. Anytime a player dove on the floor for a loose ball or took a charge, everyone—players from both teams—helped him up. And 90% of the accountability, correction, and feedback in the practice came from the players. This was what a practice was supposed to look like!

The finish to our practice had changed significantly since Sam had last seen us. I found it to be one of the most important things we did now. We finished practice with what we called a debriefing. I had read about it in respect to The Blue Angels, the naval air show group that does crazy tricks and formations in their planes. Following each practice, our guys sat in a circle of four to six and shared four things from that specific day.

1. What went well for me? What could I have done better?
2. How will I fix that tomorrow?
3. Who did I think was really good?
4. Show love: hugs, handshakes

It took about four minutes for our guys to get through their small group shares, and then we came together for our big group share. I always gave the guys an opportunity to recognize who they thought had practiced well. Then we talked about things to fix for tomorrow. We would then huddle together as a full team, and guys would go around and show each other love with handshakes they made up or hugs. At this practice, I also had them finish up with their Accountability Partner to talk about their lifter/leaner goal from Skull Session before practice. The guys headed for the showers, and Sam and I sat down to talk.

You know a true friend when they'll tell you the truth, whether you want to hear it or not. That was the best thing about Sam. If it wasn't good, he was going to tell you, but if it was good, he was going to tell you that, too. His evaluation of that practice was the perfect reflection of who we wanted to be as a team. We were on course.

CHAPTER SEVENTEEN

REGIONALS

"No matter what you do, your job is to tell your story."
–Gary Vaynerchuk

We finished the regular season with positive momentum, and headed into the tournament playing our best basketball of the season.

Every state conducts the end of the season tournament a little differently. We would have to win eight games to win the State Championship. First you have to win your sectional—usually three or four games, depending on your seed and whether or not you received a bye. Next, you would move on to one or two district games. Winning the districts puts you into the regionals with the final 16 teams in the state. There are two regional games, with the winner advancing to the state tournament and Final Four. It's a tough road, even for really good teams. It takes the right draw and a little luck to get it done.

Since we had finished the season so well, we had a good match-up in our first two games. Those games turned out to be lopsided wins that allowed our reserves to play quality minutes. Regardless of who was on the floor or on the bench, our guys celebrated each play with genuine gratefulness and appreciation for the guy next to him. As a coach, the feeling of your team losing their individual egos to the team is one of the best you can experience.

We played well and beat a good Cartersville team in the sectional final by 15. We played well again from start to finish. Cartersville had reached this point with a stifling defense that took opposing teams out of their normal offensive system. Earlier in the season, this would have caused us major issues. But at this point in the season, with this team, we never flinched. Our guys attacked with the same poise and aggressiveness we had for weeks. We jumped out to a 10-2 lead and maintained that 8-10 point lead for the entire game, finally stretching it to 15 points with free throws down the stretch. It was another solid performance that pushed our momentum into the next week of practice. The win advanced our team to the District finals for the first time in 20 years.

I always viewed the districts as a special level of the tournament. In our division, we have about 200 schools. Advancing to the round of 32 is an accomplishment for most schools. Our school was no different. We had won only one District Championship in the 74-year history of the school.

We faced a huge defensive challenge in the district final. Carter High, our opponent, had the leading scorer in the state, Boogie McGuire, a dominant player who averaged over 32 points per game. We would need to be at our best—but our guys were up to the challenge.

McGuire, 6'8" of pure muscle, was a force in the lane. He scored at will and tracked down rebound after rebound. McGuire looked like a grown man playing with middle school kids at recess. On most nights, he completely controlled the game. Our match-up for McGuire wasn't a good one on paper; not many are. Grant Crooks was a physical, 6'2" role player for us. But he had a way of getting under the most opponents' skin, leading to poor decisions and over-aggressive plays. Boogie McGuire was not most opponents, though. Boogie started the game with back-to-back dunks—not the start we were looking for, but from that point on, Grant did his thing. He frustrated McGuire for the rest of the game. Of course, for a player as good as McGuire, keeping him under control is an undertaking for the whole team, not a single player. The combination of Grant's knack for frustrating him and our other guys being in perfect position throughout the game led to major foul trouble for McGuire. His time was limited throughout the first half largely because of two charges we drew on him in the 2nd quarter.

With him out of the game, we handled them easily, opening up a 20-point lead at one point in the fourth quarter. Boogie finally fouled out of the game with 2:45 left in the game, finishing his remarkable season with the lowest output of the year: 17 points, five rebounds, four turnovers, and five fouls—a remarkable defensive performance by our team. We were headed to the Sweet 16, two games away from the State Championship.

CHAPTER EIGHTEEN

THE WATER BOTTLE

"I am not afraid of storms, for I am learning how to sail my ship."
–Louisa May Alcott

I always felt from the regionals on, every team was capable of winning the state title. To be one of the last 16 teams out of over 200 in the state, each team had to be good. This year was no different.

I couldn't have been more proud of how our guys had been playing. Unselfish, focused, disciplined, they were not taking anything for granted. They were Fight Ready. They were in before school every day to get extra ball handling reps and shots up. They approached every drill in practice with urgency and purpose, and they clearly trusted each other and enjoyed their time together. They competed like crazy in practice, challenging each other about meeting standards, while consistently acknowledging even the smallest contributions of teammates.

One of my favorite memories of the season came following our next game, the regional semi-final, when our leading scorer humbly acknowledged the contribution of a reserve player. After each game, win or lose, we did four things. We talk about how we measured up to our standards in our core values; we shared moments of greatness—times when teammates went above and beyond expectations; we had a circle of gratitude, where players shared what they were grateful for from that night or leading to that night; and we did a pushup for every turnover we had.

This memory stands out not because of what was said, but how it was said. Our leading scorer was a great player. He would've been more likely to be identified as a look-a-like for Shaggy from Scooby Doo than he would have been a high-level basketball player, which was the exact origin of his nickname: Shag. He didn't pass the looks test, but neither did our team. Make no mistake though, he could flat out play, and so could our team.

Shag was a good teammate, but he was also reserved. He didn't open up as much as some of the other guys on the team. Since we had started to pour into our core values, we'd had three or four guys break down crying in the locker room while sharing things with the team that they would have never considered sharing previously. Shag was not that guy—except on this night. We saved the grateful circle for last. Shag immediately stepped forward and asked if he could go first.

"Coach, I know everyone on the team has important roles. But I just want to let Kyle know how thankful I am for him and what he brings to this team. I know he wants to play more on Friday nights, but you would never know it by how much he encourages guys during huddles or celebrates on the bench. I mean, we go at each other in practice all the time. Sometimes I talk crap to him, sometimes he talks crap to me. But he never lets it get to him. It would be so easy for him to hate me or not root for me since we play the same position, but it's never like that," he told the group.

"Tonight, late in the 4th quarter during a timeout," he continued, and then stopped. Tears were starting to pool up in his eyes now. He tried to rub them on his shoulder as if he was wiping away sweat, but none of the guys bought it. He kept his head down.

"I'm sitting down, listening to Coach and grabbing a water bottle, but it was empty. I shook it and sat it back down. I was good, didn't really need a drink to finish out the game. A few seconds later, I feel a tap on my shoulder. It's Kyle, handing me two cups of water that he had just gone to the end of the bench to get. He says, 'Here you go, Shag. Keep playin' hard. We got this one!' I don't know what else Coach said during the rest of that timeout, but I do remember thinking, I will do anything in my power for him to win, for Kyle to get to cut down that net," he said.

I was glad to be learning this after we had won the game. Shag was incredible for the entire game, but it came down to the final possession. That wasn't much of a surprise. Our opponent was led by a 7'1" NBA-bound star. He was pretty much unstoppable, having scored 52 points a few weeks earlier. He was great in this game too, but Shag stole the show by sinking several key free throws down the stretch to ice the game. Both players ended the game scoring 32 points for their teams, but it was our West Lake Spartans that advanced to the Regional Final.

All teams have ceilings: their maximum potential. No one ever really knows exactly where that ceiling is until the dynamics of that particular team surface. One of the most telling indicators is who ends up leading the team. Will it be the coach, or will the players step forward and take ownership of the team themselves? A player-led team will always have the highest ceiling. And our players owned everything about this team—on the floor, in the locker room, in the school, and in the community.

Shag looked up now, with no effort to hide the tears running down his cheek. He looked directly at Kyle and said: "I'm so thankful to have you on my team, man. You've made me a better player and better person. You're a true foxhole dawg. I love you. If you ever need me, now or the rest of your life, I got you."

The locker room went crazy. Guys started jumping around, hugging each other, piling on Kyle. It was one of those moments that remind you why you coach.

CHAPTER NINETEEN
MAN IN THE ARENA

"Some beautiful paths cannot be discovered without getting lost."
–Erol Ozan

We only had three days between Regional games. The atmosphere in the school was electric. The hope in the community was apparent in the faces of every fan. There was a definite satisfaction in bringing that type of joy to our area.

Signs with our players' names lined the roads, cheerleaders had painted well wishes on the windows of businesses in town, and the line to buy tickets for the upcoming game at the school wound through the hallways and out the front of the building. Clearly, our community was invested in our team. Everyone I passed for the next three days wanted to talk about the team and our next opponent. At the start of the season, many had thought we would have a good season, but no one expected this group to advance further than any team in school history.

Nerves were clearly present leading up to our next game. Players walked the edge of being excited to play and nervous about what was at stake. To their credit, our practices continued to be inspired nonetheless—and our ceiling continued to rise. Every practice had the urgency of a final one.

In order to challenge our guys, we invited a few former college players in for practice during this time to provide a better look for the next opponent. One of the players was a professional player in Europe who happened to be home for a few weeks. Initially, this scout group completely dominated our guys in practice. I was interested to see how the guys would react to this new adversity. Their response told me all I needed to know about our progress.

Rather than point fingers for mistakes, the team took responsibility and vowed to correct mistakes. Failure on a defensive assignment was met with self-dissatisfaction, only to immediately be lifted by the encouragement of a teammate. High fives, low fives, pats on the backs, and meaningful conversations about the task at hand were abundant. The gym was loud but intentional and happy but focused. And more than anything else, you could tell our guys loved being with each other. Sure, they wanted to do well, but they cared just as much that their teammates performed at their best. They were as connected as any team I had ever seen.

In the locker room before the Regional Final game, the tension was palpable. It was way too tense and certainly not where I wanted us to be, emotionally or mentally, this close to game time. We had never been to the Final Four, so a win in this game would make history for our school, and I could tell the guys were feeling that pressure. I was never big on pre-game speeches in basketball. The spike in adrenaline may be a great thing in football, but in basketball it can quickly turn to over-aggressive fouls, poor decisions, and ill-advised shots. I preferred a focused, steady, locked-in but confident pregame approach. On this night, however, my team needed more from me, which I had anticipated.

We went through our normal scouting report routine, reminding guys of match-ups and our gameplan. Then I did my best to free them.

"OK, guys. I want to read you a passage that means a lot to me. My dad gave me a copy of this when I was in high school. It had nothing to do with basketball at the time, but I had been going through a stretch where I was worried about being popular, worried about what people thought of me. And it was holding me back. I hope this does for you what it did for me," I told them.

"It's called 'The Man in the Arena,' and it's a passage from a speech by Theodore Roosevelt."

"It is not the critic who counts; not the man who points out how the strong man stumbles, or where the doer of deeds could have done them better."

I stopped to look at the guys before continuing.

"Do we have any critics? Do we have people who want to see us fail so they can say 'Told you so?' You bet we do. Anyone striving for excellence will."

"The credit belongs to the man who is actually in the arena, whose face is marred by dust and sweat and blood; who strives valiantly; who errs, who comes short again and again, because there is no effort without error and shortcoming..."

"Has our face been marred? Anyone remember the beginning of the year?"

"...but who does actually strive to do the deeds; who knows great enthusiasms, the great devotions; who spends himself in a worthy cause..."

"We've been striving, right? So, is our cause worthy?

"...who at the best knows in the end the triumph of high achievement, and who at the worst, if he fails, at least fails while daring greatly..."

"And we definitely dare greatly. It's one of the things I love about you guys. You've embraced being different. You've held yourself, and each other, to standards others would never even consider."

"...so that his place shall never be with those cold and timid souls who neither know victory nor defeat."

I finished by saying, "We have no desire to be with those cold and timid souls. Forget the critics—they're not in the arena. The only opinions of you that matter are those of the 12 guys in this room. And we all know we've got each other's backs. If we win, we celebrate the triumph of high achievement. If we lose, we will do so daring greatly. It won't be because we held back or feared losing. We have no fear of that. We focus on the process and we surrender the outcome. That's what we do."

I stood to start the break.

"Tough and together on three. One, two, three, TOUGH AND TOGETHER!"

CHAPTER TWENTY

IT ALL COMES TOGETHER

"Fate whispers to the warrior, 'You can not withstand the storm.'
The warrior whispers back, 'I am the storm."
—Robert Sullivan

What. A. Game. I can't begin to take you back through all the key plays in this game, so I'll just get right to the play that sealed the win. To understand it completely, I need to tell you a little of Hitch's story.

Kevin Hitchenson—we called him Hitch—grew up in a single-parent home, and that parent—his mom—was gone most of the time. His dad left the family when Hitch was about three years old. His father spent the time between then and now in and out of jail for various drug charges. Hitch's mom made a little more effort to parent, but not much. She was also pretty involved with drugs, and couldn't keep a job. Hitch had a younger brother and sister whom he basically raised. They lived in five different houses during his freshman and sophomore years of high school—amazingly, all still in our school district.

Physically, Hitch wasn't exactly a specimen. At 6'1 and 160 pounds, he was considered small and light for the competition we had to play. Any muscle he had at the time was not from his genes, but from countless hours in the gym and weight room. I can still see Hitch sitting against the wall, all by himself, at our first open gym of his sophomore year. His floppy, curly hair and physique said that he was anything but a basketball player.

Hitch had never played organized basketball until his freshman year. Throughout middle school, he was never allowed to play because he had to take care of his little brother and sister. That never stopped him from working on his game, though. From the first time I saw him play, I could see he had put in a lot of work on his game. During his freshman year, his aunt moved to town and began helping him and his family out. She is the one who pushed him to give school basketball a try, and provided the help with his siblings he needed. His aunt was the one person in his life who genuinely cared about Hitch and his future before he entered our basketball program.

He had a good season with our freshman team. He was clearly one of the better players, but he had trouble adjusting to playing with teammates in an organized setting. During his sophomore year—he was probably only 5'8 and 145 pounds at the time—he suffered a variety of nagging injuries. Ankles, shin splints, pulled muscles... you name it, he had it. Then, just before his junior season started, he tore his ACL and was out for that entire season.

I'm sure this led to far more problems for Hitch at home than it did with us. His family had no health insurance, so getting him to a doctor and getting his surgery scheduled took months. He missed playing that entire season, but he also missed everything else associated with being on a team. His mom would not allow him to come to practices and games unless he could play. I called her several times, and tried to go to her house to talk, but it always came back to money. If Hitch couldn't play, she wasn't going to pay her sister to watch the other two kids when he could do it. Hitch was devastated. He withdrew from any interaction with me or the team out of frustration and embarrassment. I continued reaching out to him, but didn't get much back.

Hitch never allowed any of that to derail him. His senior season was his coming-out party. He showed up to everything we did in the pre-season, stayed healthy, and was our starting point guard from day one. He was a unique kid. He had no aspirations to play college ball, but you sure wouldn't know it by the way he worked at his game. He was always the first to the gym in the morning and the last out after practice every night. Some of that was relief from his home situation, but the bigger part was a genuine love for the game.

This kid had a lot stacked against him, but he had one thing going for him that can't be measured. Coaches call it heart, or the It Factor. He just had it. Whatever you call it, I knew one thing: I wanted him on my team. Any team I am on, I would want Hitch there with me. That season, he made so many plays to win games or give us a chance, I can't possibly count them all. Over and over he came through. He had the unwavering trust of everyone in our locker room, and he played with emotion. Our guys loved him for that. He epitomized our core values.

So, here's the situation: we're at the Regional Finals in triple overtime, tied at 64. Cyprus High has the ball. A win seals our school's first trip to the Final Four. A loss, and our season is over.

Everyone would acknowledge Hitch's 15 points (which was five above his season average), or his step-back jumper at the end of regulation to send the game to overtime, or the pass to Shag off a steal with 10 seconds left to send us into second overtime. Those plays were great, but the play he made with 45 seconds remaining in the second overtime was Hitch at his finest.

With the score tied at 72, Hitch was matched up with Dominique Robinson on the Cyprus High team. Robinson was an incredible player. He was Mr. Basketball—an award given to the best player in the state. He was also a consensus McDonald's All-American. With under a minute to play, Robinson attempted to hold the ball for a final shot. He pulled the ball out from the offense moving back towards midcourt. Now only about 45 seconds remained. Hitch was completely unphased by the 6'6" Robinson's superior size and speed, or the 24 hard-earned points Robinson had poured into the game. Hitch didn't flinch nor did he back up, and despite the seeming advantage for Robinson and his team, our guys on the floor mirrored Hitch's confidence. Tough!

As Robinson pulled the ball out, Hitch stayed right in his pocket, forcing Robinson to give the ball up to a teammate. Robinson scurried around a few screens, desperate to get the ball back for the final shot, but Hitch made him work, denying pass after pass until Robinson was finally able to take a handoff and settle back near midcourt.

With 18 seconds left, Robinson had to attack now. He sized Hitch up with a few between-the-legs rhythm dribbles as he worked his way closer to the three-point line. Hitch was ready for the challenge and stayed tight to the dribbler, generating a "five second closely guarded count" by the official.

One second.

Robinson gave a hard hesitation dribble in an effort to raise Hitch out of his attacking defensive stance. He didn't bite. Robinson followed his hesitation with a lightning quick insideout dribble coming back to his right. Hitch was ready. It seemed as if he knew the move was coming before Robinson did. Maybe that extra film Hitch had been watching did make a difference. Passionate!

Two seconds.

Way too talented to let that deter him, Robinson spun back to his left in a blur, all his talents on display. The crowd reacted to the phenomenal move with a loud "OOOOoooooo." With Hitch's other West Lake teammates in perfect defensive position, all he found was the relentless guard's chest. Unified!

Three seconds.

Now Robinson was starting to worry. That move should've given him the space to get off the game-winning shot, but it had only wasted another second. Unwilling to give in, Robinson tried to bounce his dribble back towards midcourt to create space and make another go at it. There was still 15 seconds left—plenty of time. A solid plan, but he did not account for the tenacity of his defender. As Robinson pulled back to avoid a violation and subsequent turnover, Hitch stayed attached, his right hand tapping Robinson's left hip like a hot stove and his eyes glaring straight through his chest.

Four seconds.

Panic set in for Robinson now. He dropped his shoulder and drove as hard as he could to his right, hoping to lose his defender or draw a foul to save him from the looming turnover, which would result in our team being rewarded possession of the ball and our own chance to win the game. Neither prevailed. Hitch stayed squarely in front of him, and on the second dribble, the screech of the official's whistle sounded.

Five seconds!

Hitch responded with a primal scream that still gives me chills today when I think about it, then turned to celebrate the play with all of his teammates. Thankful!

The pure passion, the unrelenting drive to compete against any odds—it was the best of high school sports on full display at the biggest moment of the season: our core values at their best.

He had no fear of critics. He dared greatly. We trusted the process and surrendered the outcome.

We took possession of the ball with just over 10 seconds to play in the game. I called a timeout to set up our final shot. The calm, poise, and focus of the timeout was transcendent. Our guys had just made one of the most important defensive plays in the history of our school, and were able to celebrate that play and immediately move on to the needs of the next moment.

The play we drew up was compromised when we weren't able to enter the ball where we wanted to. Fortunately, it ended up in the hands of Hitch. It would be up to him to make yet another play to win the game. He caught the ball at the far end of the floor—75 feet away with 10 seconds to play. Cyprus had decided to press us, so when Hitch turned to attack our basket, he had a defender in his face.

Hitch immediately ripped the ball low, right through his defender's outstretched arms. The inadvertent contact made no difference to Hitch as he blew by the first defender. A second defender came at him as he neared halfcourt, but Hitch was a step ahead. As soon as the defender committed to stopping the ball, Hitch snapped a pass to his open teammate on the far wing.

Immediately following his pass, Hitch cut hard to the basket and received the ball right back for a give-and-go, the oldest play in basketball. Hitch was now inside our three-point line with the ball, attacking the basket with six seconds to play. He took a lateral dribble to evade the first defender in the lane, then a hard downhill dribble to size up the lone opponent meeting him at the rim.

Eyeing the rim, Hitch elevated in what everyone in the gym thought was an attempt to score the winning lay-up. Everyone, that is, except Hitch and Shag.

Shag had been denied the ball the entire night. Cyprus had done an outstanding job on him, making it very difficult for Shag to find open shots. He had managed to grind out 18 points up to that point, but he had earned every last one of them.

This possession was no different. Cyprus was doing everything they could to keep from allowing the outcome of the game to be in his hands. Coming out of the timeout, the Cyprus defender met Shag on the sideline in a futile attempt to intimidate him. Shag stationed himself on the right side of the floor, squarely in front of our team bench, where he waited. When he realized the play was off and Hitch was improvising, he took a couple steps away from the lane to create more space for a potential drive. Shag's defender had been true to his assignment all night, never looking away from the numbers on Shag's chest—except for this one glimpse.

Just as Hitch left the ground for what appeared to be the game-winning shot, Shag's defender let down his guard for a fraction of a second. He turned his head ever so slightly to catch a glimpse of the final play. As if he knew the defender was going to look away, Shag instantly cut to the baseline and open space.

Hitch gathered the ball on his way up, absorbing contact from the Cyprus defender attempting to block his shot at the rim. In one effortless motion, Hitch, eyes squarely on the rim, raised the ball as if to take the shot—and flipped a perfect pass to the cutting Shag in the corner. Shag buried the shot as time expired.

CHAPTER TWENTY-ONE

OFF SEASON REFLECTION

*"Aspire greatly; anything less than a commitment to excellence
becomes an acceptance of mediocrity."*
–Brian Tracy

I wish I could tell you the Final Four game played out like that, but the truth is, we lost by five to the eventual champions. Our West Lake players and coaches were heartbroken, devastated. They had poured so much into each other, becoming the best possible team a group of individuals could possibly be. It hurts when you give everything you have to something and it doesn't work out the way you want it to. But I had seen the other option. I had coached teams that did it the other way—holding back, guys trying to take more for themselves than they're willing to give—and the two don't compare. I'd choose this pain and heartbreak every single time.

I cried, too. The season had changed me, and I knew one thing for sure: I never wanted to go back to coaching the way I had before. This transformation in my approach to coaching had redirected my life just as much at home as it had on the court or in the locker room. The core values of our basketball program were the core values of my life. The past few months, I had lived them.

At home, I was Tough enough to stop watching films of games or practice sessions and spend more time playing with Dink and Chubs. I played more trucks, tractors, and dress up than I had in the previous five years. And I am ever so Thankful for that. I was Passionate enough to put my family first. My alarm was set for 4:30 am every day. This was my way of putting my family in front of basketball: by doing my basketball work before anyone else was awake. Then, when they were up, I could focus on them.

It made a world of difference for me, mentally and physically. I lived the *Unified* core value by being completely present with my family. I heard their stories and I shared mine. Being fully in the moment was one of the most fulfilling benefits of living intentionally through my core values. For me, it strengthened our unity, and I started expressing my gratitude and love for my family more. I hope they always knew I loved them, but now I was sure to tell them every day. I gave more hugs and compliments. Both were out of my comfort zone, but it got easier every day.

This team is the one that helped me on that journey. I would like to think that I helped them on their journeys, too—of course as basketball players, but more importantly, as people. I hope they are better sons, husbands, fathers, and friends as a result of being a part of our basketball program. I love the game of basketball, but it's really nothing more than a platform, a place for people to learn about themselves, appreciate the differences in each other, and understand that every person adds value to the team in their own unique way. The game has so much to teach us and those we coach—but if we're not intentional about teaching those lessons, then we leave them up to chance.

I once had a very successful high school coach tell me that success is measured in State Championships: you're either a state champion, or you're nothing. While I can appreciate the drive this evokes, it doesn't align with my beliefs.

To me, success is like saying a kid who earns an A in a class is more successful than a kid who gets a B. What if the girl who got the B did everything she could to earn that grade—finished all the homework, sat in the front rows, studied every night, asked questions—while the girl who got the A did virtually nothing, but was just better at math? Does the potential of the student matter? Is the process the student takes a factor in determining success? For me, there is no question about it. Potential matters; process matters. The girl who got the A may have been more successful, but the girl who got the B experienced excellence. It became crystal clear: excellence is what I value, not success.

Excellence is a pursuit of your very best and your maximum potential. Helping others strive for excellence in everything they do gives me life. I finally put what I had felt for so many years into words: stay loyal to pursuing excellence, and the result will take care of itself. And I finally was living what I believed.

Did this team fail because they didn't win a State Championship? I suppose if that was our goal when we set out, then yes. But that was never our goal. Whatever games or championships we won were simply a by-product of the process we embraced. Trophies were never the aim; excellence was the goal. Growing in the core values, maximizing our potential, and becoming the best possible team this group could be. Many people avoid goals like this because they aren't absolute and easy to check off. Excellence is what we all should seek—excellence in our relationships, our work, and our faith. Most shy away from it, because pursuing excellence is a never-ending journey. You can never check the box. This team ran towards that challenge.

They played the game to win, with no fear of losing. We were *tough*. We were Fight Ready. Our body language never waivered. You could see it lifting not only each player, but the group as a whole. We were *Passionate*. We Stole Inches. Whether it was running to the opposite end of the floor to huddle before a free throw while the other team walked, or jogging to pick up the ball for the official after it rolled away, we did it. The extra work we put in provided us with the confidence we needed to compete at the highest level with no regard for the critics. We were *Unified*. We never flinched. Good plays, bad plays, good calls, bad calls, we stayed true to exactly who we were. We did it our way and didn't hold anything back. We were *Thankful*. We showed love. Our guys didn't just say they cared about each other; they showed it. Guys picking up teammates after charges, celebrating a play from the bench, or running on and off the floor during a substitution—we showed love. Love for our teammates, love for our school, and love for the game. We were excellent, regardless of what the scoreboard said.

It was such a liberating feeling to define success on our terms. The disappointment of not having another game together was there, but embarrassment, regret, and emptiness were not.

I was so grateful for that feeling. I was grateful for our team.

We had truly trusted the process. We had surrendered the outcome.

"If I accept you as you are, I will make you worse; however, if I treat you as though you are what you are capable of becoming, I help you become that." – Johann Wolfgang von Goethe

155

DISCOVERING YOUR CORE

"The core of your true belief is never lost.
Let go of all the pretending and the becoming you've done just to belong.
Curl up with your rawness and come home.
You don't have to find yourself; you just have to let yourself in."
—D. Antoinette Foy

LEADING THROUGH CORE VALUES

"Make no little plans; they have no magic to stir men's blood."
–Daniel Burnham

L iving your core values and surrendering the outcome is not playing hard, doing your best, or even having fun. It's not participation ribbons or trophies for seventh place. It's not winning the championship.

We don't control the outcomes we experience in life. Sometimes we do everything right and get the outcome we desire, and sometimes we don't. The thing we *can* control is the process. That's it. Fortunately, process drives results. That's surrendering the outcome.

With this in mind, our focus should be on establishing the process that will lead to the outcomes we want—which are not necessarily success as society defines it. Basing success on reaching a specific destination yields only short-term satisfaction. Of course the results are important, but they distract and blur the process for many people.

The goal of this book is to help you redefine success as growth: growth in your values and towards the person you aspire to be.

This process allows you to release the stress and pressure of achieving the recognition or status you might currently be chasing.

The process of becoming a core-value-based leader will be one of the most fulfilling journeys of your life. You will experience changes in your professional and personal life you don't expect, and you will feel the wholeness of living with true purpose and intentionality. Something magical happens when we fully live inside the person we are meant to be.

THE 4 PILLARS OF CORE VALUES-BASED LEADERSHIP

"When you know what's important, it's a lot
easier to ignore what is not."
-Marie Forleo

Here is a quick preview of the key elements of an intentional life. The next several pages will provide you with tools and activities to make this plan your own.

- Pillar 1: Self-Awareness
  - Self-reflection and self-discovery. We have the answers; we just have to be willing to look within to find them.

- Pillar 2: Purpose
  - Purpose Statement: your personal mission. Why you do what you do.
  - Core Values: the values you live, or want to live, your life by. These values make your purpose a reality.
  - Critical Behaviors: your values in action. What your core values look like at their best.

- o   Beliefs: guiding principles for how you live your life. Words you live by.

- Pillar 3: Courage
  - o   Strong Voice: learning to let your strong voice have the last word.
  - o   Green Light Mentality: how to stay positive.
  - o   Failure Recover System: establishing a habit for dealing with failure.
  - o   Personal Mantra: refocusing on what's most important.

- Pillar 4: Personal Standards
  - o   Slight Edge Concept
  - o   Complexity Challenges
  - o   Standards of Excellence Chart
  - o   Intentional Performance Plan

By understanding how to effectively lead ourselves, we are able to adjust the sails and guide our lives in the direction of our choosing (and help others do the same). Without this framework, we drift aimlessly. We may do good things and have great intentions, but our impact will be compromised without the clarity and direction we gain from a true understanding of ourselves.

PILLAR 1: SELF-AWARENESS

"As you think, so you shall become."

–Bruce Lee

This pillar is a prerequisite to identifying your purpose, core values, and critical behaviors. Time spent working on your values and purpose will be a waste of time if you don't take time first to know yourself.

Without question, self-awareness is the pillar most often missing from a leader's foundation. Far too often, excited and aspiring leaders forge ahead, living their best impression of their favorite teacher, coach, or parent. They get so busy trying to do things the way their mentor did them that they fail to ever consider what they believe. Mentorship and guidance is essential in developing as a leader, but it does not replace understanding who you are and what you believe. It is impossible to be authentic without self-awareness.

TOOLS FOR GAINING SELF-AWARENESS

The Stories We Tell Ourselves
This is more about heightening an awareness than actually doing a specific exercise. Begin to recognize the stories you tell

yourself. When a friend doesn't text you back, what story do you tell yourself about their lack of response? When someone cuts you off in traffic, what story do you use to explain their behavior? Acknowledging that you are, in fact, making up stories with very little factual data is a major piece of self-awareness. Too often we find ourselves acting on emotions we think are derived from an event or happening in our life. In reality, our emotions are the result of the story we tell ourselves about the event, not the event itself.

A few ideas to help gain this awareness:

- Nightly journaling. Spend a few minutes each night reflecting on your day and writing down the stories you told yourself throughout the day.
- Ask "What do I know for sure?" When you're thinking about something that was said or done, pause and ask yourself what you know *for a fact* about the situation.
- Recognize the process. Our feelings and resulting actions are a result of the stories we tell ourselves. Change the story and you'll change your actions. Build in time between what you see and hear and how you decide to behave to identify the story you're telling.

Good to Great Questions (from *Good to Great: Why Some Companies Make the Leap and Others Don't*, by Jim Collins)

- What are you passionate about?
- What are you really good at?

- What can you get paid for? I like to think of the last question as "How can I contribute to others, or what do I have to give?" However, the need to make a living is reality, and allows us to continue helping others.

Though these questions give great insight into our purpose (Pillar 2), the reflection required to truly answer them is the foundation of self-awareness.

Three Words

Do others see you living the values you aspire to? This is the real measure, right—living our core values, not just talking about them. Ask five people you know to share the first three words that come to mind when they think of you. They may think you're weird at first, but our goal isn't to be like everyone else— it's to be truly ourselves.

Meditation

In order to live by your core values, you have to be intentional. Living differently doesn't happen by accident. Meditation is a tool to help you live on purpose. It builds mindfulness, which we all need. There are hundreds of options out there. My personal choice is the Headspace app. The tool you choose isn't important; consistently taking time to be quiet, reflect, and focus is.

PILLAR 2: PURPOSE

"Most men lead lives of quiet desperation
and go to the grave with the song still in them."
−Henry David Thoreau

CLARIFYING YOUR PURPOSE

Purpose is why you live: why you do the things you do. It's our calling, our destiny. Purpose is a process, a way of life; it's not a destination. Our purpose is never a job title or certain house. It's not a salary or net worth, not an award or certain status. Your purpose fulfills you and makes you feel whole, like you're contributing to the good of the world. The most beautiful aspect of finding your purpose is that it can be applied to all aspects of your life. Your purpose is just as relevant at home with your family as it is at work with your co-workers. It should impact your time spent with friends as well as your time spent alone. Your purpose is about your actions, more importantly, it's about the impact you desire to have on others.

TOOLS FOR CLARIFYING YOUR PURPOSE

Level 5 Moments (from Simon Sinek's *Start with Why*)
Reflect and identify significant moments in your life. When you look back on your life, there will be major events that stand out;

they are your Level 5 Moments. Think about the lessons you learned from these moments. What were the feelings these experiences evoked? All of this reflection sheds light on the things you value the most. (See Chapter 7 for how Mick did this.)

Inside-out Coaching Questions (from Joe Ehrmann's *Insideout Coaching: How Sports Can Transform Lives*)

- Why do I coach?
- Why do I coach the way I do?
- How does it feel to be coached by me?
- How do I define success?

These questions provide great insight into your purpose and what matters the most to you. They require deep reflection and thought. Write your answers to these, don't just think about them.

Picture of Excellence

What does excellence look like? What does it feel like? When you achieve excellence, what are you doing and what is the result of your actions on others? Write down as many phrases as you can that express this. If you prefer the artistic route, draw your picture of excellence.

Writing Your Purpose Statement

Putting your purpose into words is often more difficult than putting it into action. This should be a working mission statement, something you revise until you get it just right. (Mick's dad helped him out with this in Chapter 8.)

My personal purpose statement is:

My purpose is to inspire others to strive for excellence over success.

Your purpose statement has two critical parts.

1. Your action: what will you do? What action will you take?
2. The resulting action in others: what will others do as a result of your action? How will their lives be changed?

The best format looks like this:

My purpose is to (your action/what you will do) so that others will (the desired response/how you will impact them)

Here are a few examples of clear purpose statements:

★ To inspire others to strive for excellence over success

★ To seek growth so I can move on from past experiences and help others do the same

★ To give hope so others will be moved to pursue their goals

- ★ To be kind so others are moved to live their lives free of judgement
- ★ To build connections with others in order to help them find joy in doing what they love

IDENTIFYING CORE VALUES

The path to living your purpose runs through your core values. An understanding of not only who you are, but also who you aspire to be, is vital. This process is not a short or easy one, and it is one that few undertake. It is no coincidence that you see so few people truly living their purpose in the real world. It's important to note that the goal is simplicity: you are trying to identify a few values you can be consistent in living rather than several that sound good but that you don't follow through on.

Tools for Identifying Core Values

Real-life Heroes
Identify three people in your life you admire. What values do they embody that you aspire to? Write them down and consider the core values you want to live your life by. Start big, with a list of 10-15. Narrow that list to seven or eight, then down to three or four. It's important this list is short.

24-word Eulogy
Write what you want people to say about you at your funeral. Take your time and make sure it addresses how you want to be

remembered. The challenge to keep it to 24 words or less is essential. Everyone has heard stories about the clarity death brings to life. Why not establish exactly who we want to be now, then live our life with intentionality and purpose to make it true?

Banquet Speech

Use this for younger leaders (rather than the eulogy exercise above). Write what you want your coach to say about you at your end-of-season banquet. No limit on words. I've never had a player write that they started or averaged a certain number of points. This activity always points young people to what they value, even if they have never verbalized it previously.

The Obstacle is the Way

Consider times when you have compromised your beliefs. Think about times you made a choice that didn't align with who you want to be. What excuses did you make to justify it at the time? Now, consider times when you made a tough choice that does align with who you want to be. What excuses did you ignore in order to make that tough choice?

SELECTING CRITICAL BEHAVIORS

Think of critical behaviors as small goals you hold yourself to each day. They may seem minor in the moment, but they are powerful in their cumulative impact. Critical behaviors are your core values in action. It's these small acts that fulfill you by providing the stage for your core values to come alive. (See Chapter 9 to remember how Mick narrowed down critical behaviors for his values.)

This is deep work, and requires you to call on the self-awareness you gained from the Pillar 1. It's helpful at this stage to have someone to talk to and bounce ideas off. Verbalizing your thoughts and answers to some of those activities will lead you towards clarity in your core values. Each core value has a unique meaning to you. Tapping into that personal ideal is the path to selecting the best critical behaviors for yourself. And remember, these are behaviors: things you DO!

Here are some examples of critical behaviors for some common core values.

Core Value	Critical Behaviour
Hard Worker	Stay fully present
Passionate	Make no excuses
Loyal	Tell the truth
Gratitude	Show love
Consistency	Show up
Grow	Choose discomfort
Tough	Positive body language
Dedicated	Choose extra work

There is no right or wrong critical behavior. The best ones are those that speak to your heart and move you to action.

While I prefer assigning a single critical behavior for each value that encompasses all aspects of your life, it is sometimes beneficial to begin with behaviors that you change each week, or multiple aspects to each value. This allows you to discover ways to apply your core values in various parts of your life. The examples below may seem minor in the moment, but are powerful in their cumulative impact.

- **Critical behaviors for the value of Dependability**
  - o Parent: ask your son or daughter how their day was every day after school
  - o Coach: prepare practice schedules the night before
  - o Teammate: text three teammates four days a week just to check in

- **Critical behaviors for the value of Honesty**
  - o Parent: share something interesting from the day with family
  - o Coach: meet with three players individually this week and give them accurate, critical feedback
  - o Teammate: select a teammate for practice to provide feedback, both positive and negative

- **Critical behaviors for the value of being Hard Working**
  - Parent: text kids and spouse during lunch break three days this week just to say hi
  - Coach: watch an additional two hours of film this week
  - Teammate: work out before school three days this week

- **Critical behaviors for the value of being Tough**
  - Parent: spend the first 15 minutes when home from work talking to kids and spouse
  - Coach: have two conversations this week that you have been putting off
  - Teammate: make no excuses during practice this week

- **Critical behaviors for the value of Gratitude**
  - Parent: hug and kiss kids and spouse before going to bed every night this week
  - Coach: pull three players aside each day just to tell them you appreciate their commitment
  - Teammate: text a teammate each day just to tell them you are thankful for them

Critical behaviors are your core values in action. It's these small acts that fulfill us. These critical behaviors could change weekly or be permanent—the choice is yours.

UNCOVERING YOUR BELIEFS

Now that you have your purpose, core values, and behaviors in place, it's time to start thinking about your beliefs. It may be helpful to think of beliefs as principles you choose to live your life by. Your beliefs are often what you verbalize and provide congruence between what you think, what you do, and what you say.

Here are some examples of beliefs that align with core values. Similar to critical behaviors, there are no right or wrong ways to identify a belief—it's just one that connects to you and who you aspire to be. Short, memorable phrases are usually the most effective. Think "words to live by."

Value	Belief
Tough	Fight Ready
Passionate	Steal Inches
Unity	Don't Flinch
Grateful	Give Touches
Growth	Step Forward
Curious	Fight Complacency
Thoughtful	Be Still
Consistent	Show Up
Loyal	Be Real

PILLAR 3: COURAGE

"Courage is the greatest virtue, because it guarantees all the rest."
–Winston Churchill

When it gets down to it, what you believe and what you say doesn't really matter unless you have the courage to follow through and do it. You can say you have values and standards, but if you fail to act in alignment with them, do you truly possess them, or are they just hopes and dreams you aspire to have?

You will rise and fall with your courage, not your beliefs. Your values are only as strong as your courage to live them. Courage requires you to be vulnerable. When you are courageous, you put your true self out in front for all to see. You turn your back on the critics, ignore the weak voices in your head, and go for it.

TOOLS FOR ENACTING YOUR COURAGE

Strong Voice, Weak Voice, from a video by by Brett Ledbetter (https://youtu.be/RZPv3en9iYU)
This activity is best done with others, but is effective individually as well. Write down all the phrases you say to

yourself when things are not going well, when you mess up, when you're struggling. That's your weak voice. Now, write down all the phrases you say to yourself when things are going great, you're killing it, when you're at your best. That's your strong voice.

The purpose of the exercise is to create an awareness around two concepts.

1. Everyone has both voices. World champions have weak voices, just like everyone else. They are just really good at #2.

2. You get to choose the voice you listen to. Having the courage to listen to your strong voice, even when things aren't going well, is rare. You will never eliminate the weak voice, but you can create the habit of listening to your strong voice first.

Traffic Light Mentality

This is similar to the Strong Voice activity, but sometimes resonates better for some people.

Red light is your weak voice: doubtful, questioning, self-pity, making excuses.

Green light is your strong voice: confident, sure, positive, determined.

Write down all the phrases that come to mind for each. Green Light is a great cue to yourself or those you lead to stop listening to your weak voice and start listening to your strong voice. A green wristband or some other physical reminder can also be helpful.

Failure Recovery System, from a video with Sue Enquist and Brett Ledbetter (https://youtu.be/RZPv3en9iYU)

Courageous people are unfazed by failure. They accept it as an opportunity to grow, and move forward immediately. The idea of failure can be a huge obstacle, and creating a failure recovery system can help address that problem for us. An FRS is a process or routine you *physically* go through immediately following a mistake. An FRS has three key elements: own the mistake, get present, and engage with teammates. In some situations, engaging with teammates may not be possible, but the first two always are. Here are a few examples of what an FRS might look like.

- Sports: Pat chest and say "my bad", call the number of outs in the inning, make eye contact and point to a teammate.
- Corporate: Tell a coworker who was impacted by your mistake that it was your fault. Prior to sitting back down or moving to the next task, take three deep breaths. On the exhale, release your mind from your

weak voice and intentionally choose your strong voice. Share your strong voice with a coworker.

- Any field: Hit your reset button. This combines all of these pieces into one action. When you hit your reset button, you immediately own the mistake, become present, and switch your mindset back to the positive.

Personal Mantra

A personal mantra is basically a go-to strong voice. Think about something you say to yourself or images that evoke the belief and confidence you aspire to live with. Use this saying or image as your single strong voice.

I have several mantras I use consistently. For some, I have images I like to flash in my head. I also have them saved on my phone.

- A wolf. Wolves are badass. Lions and tigers are cool, but you don't see a wolf performing in the circus. Wolves know who they are, and don't care if you like it or not. They're going to be a wolf.
- Man in the Arena. I use this one to remind myself to block out critics and to dare greatly. I want to aspire to great things and encourage those I'm leading to do the same.

- Keep Chopping. When things are good, work. When things are bad, work. This reminds me to stay loyal to all the little things that make the big things possible.

My mantra is a modification from a verse in the Bible, Job 39:19, but it became a mantra for me as a result of the final scene in *Secretariat*. "I laugh at fear, afraid of nothing. I will not shy away from the sword. I will not stand still when the trumpet sounds."

- The first phrase speaks to my faith and understanding that I am not in control, so what is there to fear?
- The second phrase addresses my willingness to take risks and be bold.
- The third phrase is a call to action. When it's time to go, I will be prepared and ready.

Here are a few examples of mantras others have found empowering.

★ Stay patient and trust my journey.

★ Stay present, enjoy the moment.

★ I am the sky. Everything else is just the weather.

★ Everything I need is within me.

★ Look through eyes of love, not judgement.

A mantra is powerful. We will all drift away from our purpose and values throughout our lives. A plan to minimize the time away is vital. A mantra is a specific strong voice that we plan ahead of time. It centers and returns us to who we want to be. Mantras are powerful and keep your most important asset—your attitude—moving in the right direction.

PILLAR 4: PERSONAL STANDARDS

"Faith is not only daring to believe, it is also daring to act."
-Wilfred Peterson

When leading others, you don't get what you demand, you get what you accept. The same is true for yourself. Personal standards are simply what you are willing or unwilling to accept from yourself. A person who is never late to an appointment isn't on time simply because they like being on time. They're on time because punctuality is a personal standard for them. It's more about them living up to a personal expectation than it is about being on time.

When you understand this idea—that you get what you accept from yourself and others—it's both empowering and freeing. You realize the power you have in your daily choices. Then there is only one question: what are you willing to accept from yourself?

TOOLS FOR BUILDING YOUR PERSONAL STANDARDS

Slight Edge Actions
The Slight Edge is a book by Jeff Olson. In it, he views life as the culmination of a series of tiny decisions and actions. While each

of those little actions may not seem to make much difference in the moment, put together day after day, year after year, they lead you to exactly where you are. A simple example is choosing your drink for lunch every day. If you choose water over soda today for lunch, it won't make that big of a difference in your life. You won't be that much healthier or feel that much better. But if you choose water over soda for every meal for a year, there will be significant health differences. As Olson states, these Slight Edge decisions are "Easy to do and easy not to do." Your choice in these seemingly small decisions controls the trajectory of your lives.

★ Identify three Slight Edge actions you can take daily to move yourself towards living your core values.

Complexity Challenges
Bill Eckstrom talks about his Growth Rings concept during his popular TED Talk. The concept is simple in theory, but very challenging in action. The lowest ring is stagnation. Nothing really happens in stagnation. Think of a creek that is blocked and just pools right in front of the dam. Mick was in the stagnation stage early in the story, when he was making excuses and justifying his subpar performance. The first ring has no flow and actually keeps us from growing.

The next ring is order. This is where things make sense. It's comfortable. You know what you're going to get. One thing leads to another, so you have predictable outcomes. Order often shows up as a plateau following efforts of improvement. Mick needed to be confronted by Sam following the first practice observation to move on from the order phase.

The third ring is complexity. Eckstrom describes this as "changed order." The environment and/or outcomes are unpredictable. This is where all growth occurs. Throughout our story, Mick spent much of his time in the complexity ring. Mick and Sam's initial lunch brainstorm around Mick's core values, or the hard truth shared with him by his mom and dad, are good examples of complexity.

The final ring is chaos. No control of anything creates chaos, where virtually no growth can take place because you enter survival mode. Chaos will sometimes push us back into complexity because of the discomfort it causes. This was the case for At the beginning of the story, when Mick lost his composure with his daughter Rachel, he was in chaos.

The skill here is to enter the complexity ring as much as possible. You can get to the complexity ring by being forced there by someone else (a coach, a leader, a teammate), or an event (not getting a job, failing on a project, losing a game), or you can choose to go there on your own.

Most of us stay in the comfort ring until something forces us out of it. Creating a system to regularly move yourself and your teams to complexity is a huge act in courage and step towards excellence.

★ Make a list of choices you can make to enter the complexity ring daily. Commit to getting out of your comfort zone in some area of your life each day. Identify three friends or teammates you have who can knowingly push you into complexity from time to time.

Standards of Excellence Chart

A Standards of Excellence chart is a constant reminder of who you want to be. It's a simple way to see your beliefs, critical behaviors, and core values as a constant reminder to be intentional with your life. In addition, by posting it publicly, you are much more likely to follow through. Of course, you will need to do the tough work of identifying your core values, critical behaviors, and beliefs first.

STANDARDS OF EXCELLENCE		
Belief	Behavior	Value

Intentional Performance Plan

If you rotate your Critical Behaviors, it's important to track your progress. There are hundreds of apps available to help move behaviors to habits. Regardless of what you use, it's critical to create consistency in your actions. Personally, I prefer the old-school, written approach to tracking habits. Below is an example of a format that has worked well for me.

My Intentional Performance Plan
Live on Purpose.

Why: to inspire others to strive for excellence over success

Date: July 30

Core Value 1	TOUGH "Fight Ready"							
Critical Behavior 1	I will get out of bed on my first alarm every day this week.	X	T	X	X	X	Sa	X
Critical Behavior 2	I will arrive 30 minutes before practice 4 days this week.	X	X	W	Th	F	X	Su

Core Value 2								
Critical Behavior 1		M	T	W	Th	F	Sa	Su
Critical Behavior 2		M	T	W	Th	F	Sa	Su

DISCLAIMER

"The reward for conformity is that everyone likes you but yourself."
- Rita Mae Brown

I n previous sections, I've shared several examples and ideas for purpose statements, core values, critical behaviors, beliefs, and mantras. Forget about those. Dive into self-reflection and discover your own. Perhaps you will uncover some that I've listed or one will really resonate with you; if so, please use it. The critical piece is that you came to that conclusion through your own introspective work and reflection. You can't beg, borrow, or steal these core beliefs. You have to own them.

TO PARENTS

"Do not educate your child to be rich.
Educate him to be happy, so when he grows up,
he'll know the value of things, not the price."
- Unknown

Your family is your most important team. Take the time to go through this exact same process together to establish core values for your family. Follow those values up with a critical behavior for each, and revisit them each night to check on your progress as a family.

At a minimum, plan to include your spouse in identifying the core values for your home. I also encourage you to help your children identify two core values of their own: what they believe in and who they want to be. Depending on their age, it may be important to rephrase a few of the questions to focus more on who they admire or look up to rather than self-reflection.

One of the most significant benefits of children identifying core values is helping them apply those values to school, sports, and groups of friends. These values become their barometer for success—not their grade card, playing time, or popularity—but only if you guide and help your kids use them that way!

TESTIMONIALS

"You will teach them to fly, but they will not fly your flight.
You will teach them to dream, but they will not dream your dream.
You will teach them to live, but they will not live your life.
Nevertheless, in every flight, in every life, in every dream,
the print of the way you taught them will remain.
- Mother Teresa

Floyd Lowry | Graham High School | 2013
The core values have made a huge impact on my life, not only in athletics but as a man. After graduation and moving on to college athletics, I found it very important to stay true to the core values instilled in me: be HUMBLE, be PASSIONATE, be UNIFIED, be a SERVANT, be THANKFUL. I feel as though these words have come to define me as I grew through the program and beyond.

Finally, without these core values I do not believe I would be where I'm at today. Currently I am pursuing a Doctor of Physical Therapy degree, and without these core values I would not have made it through the first semester, let alone the first year. Without being humbled and learning from each situation, being passionate and knowing this is what I want to do, being unified and knowing when I need to rely on others, being a servant and helping someone become better at a task through constructive criticism, and finally, being thankful for the opportunity while being able to continue to grow and help others. It's more than about the now, it's about what's beyond and how it can transform and impact lives beyond sports.

Kevin Meiners | Centerville High School | 2016
I will forever be grateful for the core values and principles instilled in me through this program. A team centered on core values sets its players up for success long after they are done playing basketball. I have been involved in many things since graduating high school in 2016; however, playing organized basketball was not one of them. That does not mean, though, the lessons taught to me are no longer relevant. Being tough, passionate, unified, and thankful are things we should strive to display and embrace every day. Our coaches were more concerned with coaching the person than they were with coaching the player. If all they taught us to do was to shoot better or set better screens, then they would have come up short. Instead, they taught me how to be thankful for everything God has given me. For the people who love me and care for me and for the opportunities that I have. They showed me the importance of being passionate about what I am doing. Without a passion, when things get tough and adversity hits, I will be long gone. This is a passion in all aspects, for the people I work

with as well as for the mission and vision behind what I am doing. They showed me that a unified front with whoever I am going into battle with is of the utmost importance. We would have never achieved the success we did my senior year had we not all been bought in.

The coaches knew that was going to be a process and steered us in the right direction, ultimately allowing us to buy in willingly rather than forcing us. Lastly, they taught me the importance of toughness. Life is life, and it is going to throw you curveballs and knock you down at times. Running sixes and suicides and doing track workouts in the fall were never easy, although they were necessary— to build our physical endurance, but also to build our mental endurance. They knew that us breaking on the track, overcoming it and finishing the workout would lead to us not breaking on the court. They showed us that our ability to handle adversity and conquer adversity was what sets apart the good from the great. All of these core values related to basketball, but they also relate to whatever and wherever I may go down the road. They have already helped me tremendously over the last four years, and I have no doubt they will help me in the years to come, and for that, I am so thankful!

A quick memory I have is of the Skull Sessions we would do before practice. I think about the culture that has been established within the Centerville Basketball program, and it astounds me. I believe that a huge part of that happened in those Skull Sessions. Those are an opportunity to step back from the game and learn life lessons that are universal. To talk about things that are so crucial to being successful at any level.

One specific one from my senior year stands out. We had just lost on senior night in what was a very winnable game. Our record was now 12-9 after starting 5-0. Any normal coach would have thought we need to get on the court for three hours and fix everything that is wrong. Not our coach, though; we spent over an hour in his classroom talking. He was never afraid to challenge us and hold us accountable to the standard that was expected of us. I believe that Skull Session was the turning point for us. We went on to advance to the Elite 8 after a 12-10 regular season record. Some people may say it was a lucky run, or we just caught fire at the right time, but I believe it was a result of the previous eight months, the time spent cultivating those core values and our team's resiliency and toughness that propelled us on that run. Coach Cupps understands the importance of a culture and of core values, and as a result I do, too!

Sam Fowler | Centerville High School | 2013
The core values instilled in me have played an instrumental role on how I try to live my life today. Other than my parents, no one has had a bigger influence on my life than Coach. He taught us

players that The Game Honors Toughness and that the toughest teams win.

One of the memories I have from that season which demonstrates that toughness, and that I reflect on often, was one of our first team scrimmages of the year. We played 10 10-minute quarters. We all wore plain white t-shirts, because we had not earned the right to wear our practice jerseys yet. The scrimmage ended and we had not performed well. We got back to the high school around 10:00 pm and we immediately went straight to the gym to practice ... hard. Coach and all of the assistant coaches practiced with us. Most of the coaches were in better shape than we were, which demonstrated their lead-by-example philosophy. Additionally, that reinforced what I believed in, that players are a reflection of their coaches. We finished up around midnight and we were all completely exhausted. I remember thinking that there is no way any other high school team is doing what we are doing. No way any other high school team is working as hard as we are working. This is something I have tried to live by whether in school, sports, or business—being relentless in the pursuit of excellence and finding an excuse to win. TGHT.

Matt Pearce | Centerville High School | 2019
Playing basketball at Centerville will always serve as one of the most developmental time periods of my life, in terms of not only

basketball, but life as a whole. The dedication towards our core values of being Tough, Passionate, Unified, and Thankful highlight the embodiment of important leadership characteristics that many lack nowadays. Day in and day out, our coaches showed true heart and commitment towards us, all for our benefit and growth, thus displaying their unmatchable selflessness and respect for the game. These core values have maintained worth throughout my life today, and I always find myself examining my actions and decisions on the basis of how they fit in with being tough, passionate, unified, and thankful.

A memory that stands out to me during my time playing was my senior season at Centerville. Any typical person may look at our team that year and immediately evaluate our performance by our 22-6 record (tying the school record for most wins in a season) and think we must've been all right. However, so much more goes into a basketball season than your record, and paying attention to the small little details that numbers can't explain are what made playing for Coach so much more valuable to me. Preseason, we realized we were loaded with athleticism and talent, and some teammates even hinted at the possibility of a state championship. Yet that's easier said than done, and we started with a whopping record of 4-5, which served as a huge punch in the face.

For most teams, starting this bad with the talent and capabilities we knew we possessed deflates morale and sends the season spiraling into disaster. But someone like Coach doesn't coach most teams. His guidance and leadership allowed us to build off of the disaster we started, have the crucial emotional conversations we needed to have, and turn ourselves in the right direction. He instilled in us the notion of trusting the process, and seemed somewhat happy we had started so horribly, because that's what inspired us to approach things at a whole new level. Everything fell back on the basis of our core values, and our performance in practice, games, and class was always evaluated against the standard of, "Is that something a Centerville basketball player would do? Is that specific action representative of being tough, passionate, unified, and thankful?"

Having Coach there as an epitome of holding yourself to a high standard and staying true to your values is what allowed us to turn that 4-5 start into a 22-6 finish. While many may see that transformation as simply a school record-breaking 18-game win streak, I see it as a life lesson that I will cherish forever and it all couldn't have been possible without core values and the progressive, optimistic initiative of Coach.

Adam Velasco | Centerville High School | 2017

As I went through my first two years in the program, I started to learn what it meant to be a part of the Centerville basketball program. Coaches and upperclassmen in the program taught me what it meant to embody the core values of the program.

Being a part of a program focused on core values gave me the opportunity to grow and provided an outlet for others to aid that process. Because of being part of a program committed to being tough, passionate, unified, and thankful, I was surrounded by upperclassmen who, because they were thankful for the people who came before them, chose to invest in me so I would do the same for the generations to come. This looked like the best player on varsity my sophomore year choosing to work out with me, a JV player who didn't get a lot of time on the court, every morning before school. Aside from Joey being a good guy, this is what thankfulness looks like. It was his way of saying thank you to the person who chose to invest in him by doing the same for someone else.

Playing on a basketball team where core values are the priority allowed me to learn a lot more than basketball that would carry over into my life. Other than being able to give out buckets in pick-up games in college, knowing how to read a screen and attack a close out won't do me a lot of good post-high school basketball, but the majority of what I learned from being on the

Centerville basketball team will. I learned that part of being passionate is putting in work others are not willing to put in. I learned how to wake up before my competition and out work them. I learned how to set my ego and comfort zone aside and tell the people I am thankful for in my life that I am thankful for them and that I love them. I learned that being with a group of people who come together, have genuine care for one another, and will do whatever they have to do to help the group succeed is when they will reach their potential, and I learned that the people who win in life show up and get it done, regardless of what excuse is available.

Josh Schuler | Graham High School | 2009
I truly believe being on a team centered around core values helped me prepare and adapt for life in high school, and more importantly, still in life today better than anything else I've been a part of.

The impact it has starts immediately. I had been on teams my whole life and we always had fun and had a bond. Once you are on a team centered around the same core values, that bond and respect for each other is different than anything you've been a part of. Every action you take is to work towards the same goals as a group, not for yourself. Will it always be perfect? No. But knowing you are all striving for the same values is the best way to get back on track. The people I played with and I still reference the core values to this day, and I'm forever thankful for that bond.

Post-high school is when I really saw how much it helped me in life. These values are something you can enforce to help you with family, friendships, and anyone you meet in life or in your place of work. Having them in the back of my head when approaching any situation, I believe set me on a good path. Be HUMBLE in the work you're doing. In a world of negativity, be humble and don't shoot others down. Be PASSIONATE about what you're doing and attack everything confidently. Be a SERVANT to help others when they need it. Be UNIFIED and know that you can get more done together than individually. And the one I took away more than any is to be THANKFUL. Be thankful to your family, to your friends, and for everything you have in this life.

As important as it is to live by these, try to find someone you know who can hold you accountable to these as well. Coach Cupps has been a mentor to me since the 2nd grade, and even without talking about these values until I was in high school, I believe he has been teaching me these since then. Having someone to go to that you feel confident is striving for the same values is extremely beneficial. I'm extremely thankful I've always been able to go to him and rely on him for that.

Grant Hall | Graham High School | 2012

Playing basketball on a team centered on core values is different than just playing on any basketball team. A team centered on core values is more than just words or phrases painted on the locker room walls, it's more than just cliche things like "Word of the Day" or "Phrase of the Week." Those ideas just scratch the surface. A team centered on core values is a team that lives their lives through these core values. An individual who carries themselves with the highest character, especially when no one is looking.

One speech that Coach shared with our team that I will never forget was Theodore Roosevelt's "Man in the Arena." He shared this speech during one of our Skull Sessions before a practice. In summary, Roosevelt's speech gives credit "to the man who is actually in the arena," who goes through struggles, but "who at the worst, if he fails, at least fails while daring greatly, so that his place shall never be with those cold and timid souls who neither know victory nor defeat." When I read the last part of his speech, I usually get goosebumps because it's so powerful. Basically, those that criticize someone should not be entertained because the critic doesn't know the blood, sweat, and tears that have been invested.

I have to give credit to my parents and family for raising me the way they did, but I do owe Coach for mentoring me throughout my high school career and beyond. Coach doesn't just focus on preaching core values to the team, he teaches the coaching staff the exact same way, so that they, too, can share the messages.

On the team that I played for, I was not the 'star athlete' or the guy who was going to score many points, but Coach enabled me to lead from the bench. This is where I grew the most, because it's difficult for someone to not be in the spotlight, but he always taught us that we all played a role on the team regardless if we scored 20 points, or 2 points. One of my fond memories was during one of our games towards the end of the season and it was getting down to the wire. I always sat next to Coach Setty, one of our assistants, and I was telling him what I would do or who I would sub in based on who was playing well or matchups or what the team needed most. Coach looked at the bench, asking for Setty's advice, and instead I pitched in and gave him my opinion. He said, "AAre you sure?" I confirmed my decision, and he listened to what the 17-year-old high schooler had to say. I will always remember this because Coach treated his #1 and #12 guys the same. That's what it truly means to be a leader who surrenders their actions to their core values.

Austin Jones | Graham High School | 2009
I had the pleasure of playing for Coach from 2005-2009, and was challenged to be a better man every time I stepped on the court. During my first year, we focused mainly on basketball.

Coach is a student, much like me, and we were committed to knowing and understanding everything we could about the game together.

As I got older, the focus broadened beyond basketball. He believed that building stronger character in young men yields stronger basketball players. It mattered less how well we could shoot or pass, and more that we understood the essence of teamwork and brotherhood. Coach worked tirelessly to help us bond, whether it be over our mutual frustration with a workout or the joy we found in seeing us succeed together.

Coach taught five principles back then: Humility, Servitude, Passion, Unity and Thankfulness. At the time, we studied these principles to help improve our game, but what I realized many years later is how critical these same principles are in my adult life. An awareness and commitment to these principles changes the way I see the world. I'm a better son, brother, coworker, boss, mentor, and friend as a result. These results, however, are guaranteed only through repetition. When I've strayed from these principles, greater, avoidable challenges arise.

The first principle has proved to be most important to the success of my life. Humility to me is defined as a clear recognition of who and what I really am. Followed by a sincere attempt to become what I could be. It's a continued exercise in staying right-sized. My older brother, who also played for

Coach, reminded me once that all the greatest things that have happened in my life are a direct result of me demonstrating humility; conversely, every moment of terrible frustration is preceded by my arrogance. What I both love and hate about this principle is the inevitable, endless work it requires. There's no finish line or certificate or trophy that declares I'm humble. There is simply a single day ahead where I'm forced to choose humility or not, and the more times I choose correctly, the greater impact I have on the world. This has helped me find professional success I once thought impossible, graduate from a prestigious school, travel across the world, and be a better son, brother and friend to those closest to me.

Coaching provides a fertile ground to instill these types of principles in young players. In high school, at a time when the world seems small and so few of life's real challenges are apparent, learning to play basketball with a principled foundation opens doors for personal growth later on. I'm fortunate to live an abundant life 11 years after playing for coach, and I attribute most of my success to his relentless pursuit to help me align my worldview with these principles.

Casey Crable | Graham High School | 2010
I've had the opportunity to be a part of many teams throughout my life. Most of them all follow the same script, but none of them were established around a set of core values. That was

until I started playing for Coach. When you instill those same core values into everything you do on and off the court, they become more of a lifestyle. You don't necessarily realize it right away, but the moment you're asked to look back at all you've been through (like this very moment, 10 years later) it comes to light. They're something that holds meaning that you've helped shape your very own life out of after sports are over.

As you'll read through the previous players stories and experiences, you'll notice similarities. What I would like to add is the culture created through his own character and through the core values he centers his teams off of. When you can get a group of guys to buy into them and they are willing to learn, you'll accomplish great things. I've never been on a closer team of guys than back then. The bond that we created together will last a lifetime. When you can create that type of atmosphere, you'll have a group of guys that'll do anything to accomplish a common goal.

I greatly appreciate the lessons and values I've learned from you, Coach. Thanks again.

Kyle Dodson | Centerville High School | 2015
Centering a program around a few core values goes so much farther than a simple team slogan or phrase. In my experience playing in our program, our core values were a focus in every drill, workout, film session, practice, game, etc. Everything we

did individually or as a team served a bigger purpose than just becoming a better basketball player. This aspect of Centerville Basketball and the mentorship of Coach and his staff is where I can attribute most of my success on and off the basketball court.

This program transforms its players into the best player/version of themselves, and this goes far beyond basketball. Personally, the same core values that Coach and his staff instilled in me are what secured me a job at a company that I see myself at for the rest of my working career. The same toughness and passion it took to get through a hard workout or wake up to work out before school is what got me through difficult projects and allowed me to out work other prospects.

Kyle Fedewa | Centerville High School | 2016
For me personally, I never truly realized the power that having a core set of values and beliefs can have on you until after my last year playing. When you are surrounded by a team of guys with the same core values, it becomes much easier to hold others accountable and work towards a common goal.

It wasn't until I was off to college and on my own that I really discovered how I could be self-led through developing my own core values. This is the magic behind our program. In the real world, facing any kind of adversity becomes much easier when you are confident in who you are and what you believe in.

If I could take away one thing from Centerville Basketball, it's that I truly began to understand what it takes to be successful in life and how hard one needs to work in order to reach great success. I'll never forget the days during the season where this sequence of events would happen: we would have a game on a Tuesday night, I'd go to bed around 11:00 pm after the game, and then usually around 2:30 am I'd get an email from Hudl saying we have new film available— showing that Coach had been cutting and editing it for hours after just coaching a game. A few hours later, I would tiredly walk into the gym to work out around 6:00 am, and Coach would have already been finished with his lift and was back to coaching ... and then to a full day of teaching ... and then to another practice ... and then repeat. I'll know I've found my calling in life when I can operate at anywhere near that capacity. TGHT.

Mitch Balser | Centerville High School | 2015
Coach moving to my high school my sophomore year may have been one of the single most impactful things to happen in my life. At first it was all about finding who was willing to put in the effort, and that effort pushed everyone to their limits. But that was also when I first was able to experience what would end up becoming such a key part of my life. From the beginning we drilled the importance of the core values in basketball, but, I never expected I would practically recite them in my sleep as a senior. The core values I learned from playing for Centerville

continue to impact my life today. In fact, they hang on a sticky note underneath my computer at work. I first learned what it meant to believe in the core values through basketball, but it wasn't until after basketball that I learned the true importance of them.

During the countless hours of basketball practice, breakfast club workouts, film sessions, etc. I was able to learn more and more from Coach, and what it meant to live your life through core values. He taught me what it meant to be Humble and to know what it means to appreciate where you have been, and the people that have gotten you to where you are. I have learned to appreciate the things I have been given, and those people who have put the work in before me, to help lead me towards success. I learned from him what it meant to be a Servant by watching him lead and always putting others before himself. He taught my teammates and I that the best way to accomplish your goals is together, which helped us learn the values of passion. Passion for what you love, and the passion for those who you get to experience it with. He helped create bonds and memories for us that will last me a lifetime, and helped establish a simple way of life for me: be HUMBLE, be PASSIONATE, be UNIFIED, be a SERVANT, be THANKFUL. We learned that it didn't matter the odds, if we do what we do and focus on our values, we would come out on top. I think the chemistry my team was fortunate enough to have was a large factor in our successes, and that never would have been possible without Coach.

I have a lot of particularly good memories, but one that sticks out the most to me is when we had our final day of conditioning my senior year. We were outside for our final two-hour workout that happened to be in the rain, hail, snow, and sleet. We were bundled in hats, gloves, and winter gear suitable for a workout in those conditions, and we each had our AP, Accountability Partner, we competed with. Some of the things we had to do included backwards army-crawling a football field, spider-man push-ups the length of the football field, fireman carries, backwards bear-crawls up the hill—I could go on, but basically, anything to push our bodies to the limit. The reason this sticks out is because not only was it tough, but it was the fact we went through it together as a team and it was the last time my group of guys would ever do that. It was the final test, and the feeling you had after this was completed is something you can never replace. I never thought about it until after, but that was the day I realized we brought all of our values into one workout. It was an irreplaceable experience, and it is something I miss every day.

Andrew Case | Centerville High School | 2013
Although I only had the privilege to play for Coach and his staff for one year, the lessons I learned stayed with me well beyond

basketball. First of all, the only way to be the best is through hard work and dedication. If you are not willing to outwork your opponent, not only in a game but the time leading up to it, you are not going to be successful and don't deserve to be.

When it comes to my memories of that sole season, it is filled with many more practices with sprints, film study, and competitive scrimmages than any game. Knowing your role has been the lesson that has affected my life more than anything else and has brought the mentality and teamwork I learned from Coach to everyday life. Knowing your role is important in everything from a basketball team to a large organization—such as the military, which I entered immediately after high school. On the first day of boot camp, we were woken up at 4:30 am to start our physical training for the day. When the drill instructor gathered us around him, he told us every day before we would leave our dormitory we would fall in formation. He would have us yell at the top of our lungs one simple phrase, "Lead, follow, or get out the way." Little did he know at that time, but Coach had already instilled that mentality by not only the way he spoke, but by the way he acted. Lastly, practicing what you preach is something that Coach never talked about directly, but something he exemplified each and every day. As my time with Coach was short, I learned many lessons that have shaped how I live my life and helped develop me from a high school basketball player to a young man. Chop chop!!

Ben Rosenberger | Graham High School | 2009

Coach altered the course of my life. When I was 16 years old, I decided to transfer high schools. Little did I know it was going to be a move that fundamentally changed my thought process, work ethic, and character.

When I moved to Graham High School, they had an up-and-coming basketball program led by a coach who had values. I expected to get "Xs and Os" and a playbook. What I did not expect was to be challenged. The kind of challenge that peels you away, layer by layer, from your comfort zone, breaking down the person I was and helping me to become the person I had always envisioned for myself.

Coach had a way of allowing me to realize that I already had the answers to the questions I was asking. One memory that sticks out to me is a subtle but small gesture that I will never forget. I was brand new to Graham High School. I arrived at school early, parked in the back parking lot, and walked in the building, past the gym and then past Coach's office, each morning. One morning, as I walked by his office, he walked out at the same time as me. He said, "Benny!" like he still does to this day. "You know ... I'm here every morning at 4:30 am, and the gym is open if you ever want to better your game. It's up to you." He shrugged his shoulders and walked on down the hallway, knowing he had put the ball in my court. That little nudge was enough to spark the motivation I needed to show up in the mornings before school with a purpose.

Coach understands how to motivate. And what's special about his motivational abilities is that he knows every person is different. And he finds ways to squeeze every ounce of potential into something tangible. As long as you're willing to put in the work and show up, he will give you everything he has and always have your back. And he does all of this through core values. I use all of the core values still today and they have gotten me to where I am now. I still embody those "falcon five" core values on a daily basis.

Fast forward a few years. I'm in college, and Coach asks me to help on his coaching staff at a new high school where he was hired. Before he even discussed what I would be doing, I said yes, because I know his system and his values and I know what type of person he is, and I wanted to be a part of it. Little did I know he would again be teaching me and challenging me as I tried to coach one of his middle school teams.

We formed a bond over the years and became great friends. Whenever I have life questions or am unsure of how to approach something in life, I know I can come to him for advice, and I know he will tell me what I need to hear, not always what I want to hear. It's neat to think I am just one of hundreds that have been affected in such a positive way by his teachings and friendship.

ACKNOWLEDGEMENTS

"It's not happy people who are thankful;
it is thankful people who are happy."
- Unknown

Bets for being my biggest fox hole partner, always supporting me, accepting my introverted ways, and always making me smile.

Dink for being my biggest fan, for all the scouting trips and shot charts, and for your willingness to always do you.

Chubs for sharing the game with me, for allowing me to push you more than you thought was needed, and for living your core values daily.

Mom for showing me what unconditional love looks like.

Dad for your humility, hard work, and changing the course of our family.

Johnny for being a great role model and for being yourself with no apology.

Climber for challenging me to be better, for telling me the truth, and for always looking to grow.

Buddy for the crazy workouts together and for always trusting and believing in me.

E for being a foxhole friend that always has my back, for being a great role model for Ally and Gabe, and for doing all the stuff for our programs that I don't like to do.

Coach Zeller for modeling poise on the sideline and a willingness to never stop learning.

Stephey for consistently challenging and pushing me to be better.

Grandpa Jordan for doing what you do the way you do it, and never apologizing for it.

Coach Casey for instilling a love for basketball in me as a 7th grader that has never faded.

Jeff Goddard for embracing your position as a role model and never letting your standards waiver.

Larry Greer for sharing your knowledge and mindset around the game of basketball with a little 'ol high school coach.

All players, past and present, for trusting me, sacrificing for each other, and believing in our values.

North Coast Blue Chip guys for five great years of unforgettable experiences, laughs, and friendships.

Ryan Hawk for encouraging me to write this book. I would have never made it all the way to this point without your encouragement.

Joe Neikirk and Nicci Bosco for being early proofreaders and honest critics. Your feedback was powerful in keeping this project moving forward.

Daniel Milligan for the first round of actual, professional editing. You were so easy to work with.

Mary Beth Conlee for the second and third round of professional editing. Your suggestions and attention to detail were so helpful and impactful.

Anna Demos for your creative ideas around the book cover design.

Puckett for continued encouragement and discussions around all things leadership-related.

Steven Gallagher for trusting in me and always helping me to keep the main thing the main thing.

Rex Brooking for unwavering support and willingness to make our basketball program part of his life... and for the Chic-fil-A, of course.

Mike Holweger for being an example of what a positive mindset looks like and for his continuous thoughts on basketball, life, and coaching.

Setty for your selfless support of me and our basketball programs at Graham and Centerville.

Zach Christensen for your trust and loyalty, and for stretching me out of my comfort zone by asking questions other people don't.

Troy Stoller and Chuck Cowgill for buying into our program and pushing it through our Hustle program.

Coach Goodwin for instilling a different level of toughness in me than I realized I had.

Coaching Fraternity for all you do for kids that goes unacknowledged, and especially to those coaches at schools that may not win state titles but never waiver in their commitment to their players.

Matt Middleton and Keith Cunningham for being my best friends throughout high school. I realize now how much our time together growing up has made me the person I am.

Charlie McMahan for sharing your time with me and showing me how a person of faith can still compete and strive for excellence.

Ricky for being a foxhole guy and for constantly seeking growth.

Adversity for everything. I'm tougher because of you. I'm more passionate because of you. I'm more unified because of you. And I'm more thankful because of you. I will continue to hunt and embrace you. ChopChop!